In *Tune My Heart to Sing Thy Grace,* Paul Clark has crafted a powerful book on congregational singing. Writing out of a heart that has been richly shaped by God's mercy, Clark provides a roadmap through the story of song in the Bible and church history. From years of consultation with churches, he offers sage advice for how individuals and churches can "retune" their singing. I needed the "retuning" this book provided — and you probably do too!

Dr. Reggie Kidd, Professor of New Testament, Reformed Theological Seminary, Faculty member, Robert E. Webber Institute for Christian Worship, and author of *With One Voice: Discovering Christ's Song in Our Worship*

"Paul Clark is a church musician who is equally committed to the glory of God, the building up of his church, and using the best of creativity of the past and present to look towards the future. I cannot recommend him highly enough."

Keith Getty, Christian artist, lecturer, and modern hymn writer including songs such as *In Christ Alone, Speak, O Lord,* and *You're the Word of God the Father*

Dr. Paul B. Clark Jr. provides us with a well written and thoroughly researched plea for worship renewal through congregational singing. *Tune My Heart To Sing Thy Grace* provides both a corrective and encouraging message for the church. I highly commend this book to pastors and worship leaders who are committed to building community and nurturing faith-formation among those they lead in worship.

Dr. Frank R. Lewis, Senior Pastor, First Baptist Nashville, Tennessee

Your copy of Paul Clark's *Tune My Heart...* will soon become worn, dog-eared and dirty. He has given us a book that is reliable in two important, sometimes adversarial, arenas: academics and practice. His research is broad, his focus is clear, his experience is rich, his thesis is biblical, and his mind, like his heart, is open. We must move forward in matters of congregational song and singing. With this book, Paul Clark joins those in the lead.

> Terry W. York, DMA. Professor of Christian Ministry and Church Music, Truett Seminary, Baylor University, Author of *American Worship Wars* and co-author of *The Voice of Our Congregation*

"Worship involves a rhythm of revelation and response, and this book beautifully reflects that reality. Paul Clark reveals biblical, theological foundations for radically God-centered worship, and then he gives us clear, practical guidance for how God's people respond congregationally to God's greatness. I wholeheartedly recommend this book for pastors, worship music leaders, and Christians who long to see God-honoring, Christ-exalting, Spirit-led worship in the church."

> David Platt, PHD, Senior Pastor, The Church at Brook Hills
> Birmingham, AL

Tune My Heart *to Sing Thy Grace*

Worship Renewal through Congregational Singing

Paul B. Clark, Jr.

CROSSBOOKS PUBLISHING

CrossBooks™
A Division of LifeWay
1663 Liberty Drive
Bloomington, IN 47403
www.crossbooks.com
Phone: 1-866-879-0502

First published by CrossBooks 6/4/2010

ISBN: 978-1-6150-7204-0 (sc)

Library of Congress Control Number: 2010905806

Printed in the United States of America
Bloomington, Indiana

This book is printed on acid-free paper.

Contents

Foreword vii

Prelude xi

Acknowledgments xv

Chapter 1 Needing A Worship Tune-Up 1

Chapter 2 Biblical, Theological, And Historical Foundations For Singing Worship 15

Chapter 3 Unison And Harmony – Not All Worship Gatherings Are Alike 39

Chapter 4 Words We Sing In Worship 53

Chapter 5 Music We Sing In Worship 67

Chapter 6 Sunday Worship – Time For Singing 87

Chapter 7 Sacred Acts – Sacred Singing 101

Chapter 8 Renewed Singing – Renewed Worship 117

Chapter 9 Rehearsal For Singing 141

Chapter 10 Staying In Tune 151

Selected Sources 157

Foreword

I have always enjoyed participating in worship services when Paul Clark has served as the worship leader. Many know of Paul Clark as a talented musician with a great heart for the people of God. Now, through this marvelous book that you hold in your hands, people will know of Paul Clark as a gifted writer and insightful thinker regarding matters of corporate worship.

My testimony will be the word of many others as well, of that I am sure. This fine book will enable people to think afresh about the importance of worship, the place of music in worship, and particularly the role of singing in the midst of congregational praise. In the first half of the twentieth century, W. T. Conner, the influential Baptist theologian, claimed that:

> The church is the body of Christ. He is its inner life . . . . The function of the church is to embody the life of Christ and to manifest their life to others . . . . The church cannot carry out its function of manifesting Christ except as the church is filled with the Spirit of God . . . . The first business, then, of a church is not evangelism, nor missions, nor benevolence, it is worship. The worship of God in Christ should be at the center of all else that the church does. It is the mainspring of all the activity of the church.[1]

1 W. T. Conner, The Gospel of Redemption (Nashville: Broadman, 1943), 276-78.

Reading Paul Clark has once again confirmed for me that Conner's reflections were right on target. Clark calls for the churches to recognize their need for a worship tune-up. After these reflections on the need of the hour, he offers helpful guidance for the place of congregational singing in worship based on biblical, theological and historical foundations. Some of the most helpful commentary is found in Clark's analysis of the place of both the words and the music that we sing, including the place of unison and harmony. I personally found the thoughts about renewal in singing and worship to be heartening and encouraging. The full-orbed perspectives on the place of music, variety, and sacred singing are as insightful as they are timely.

Worship, though primary in the life of the church, is often elusive and misunderstood, and in recent years has been the source of division in Baptist churches. Clark's book will be the first step for many to help remedy this situation. He calls his readers afresh to consider the primacy of worship and what it means to ascribe worth to God in his presence with our voices and our hearts.

TUNE MY HEART TO SING THY GRACE is in many ways a rightful heir of the work of the great Baptist leader, Benjamin Keach, who in 1691 penned THE BREACH REPAIRED IN GOD'S WORSHIP. In that book, Keach advocated the careful composition of sermons, prayers, and hymns, and in that same year put together the first hymnbook ever to be used by British Baptists. The hymnal, SPIRITUAL MELODY, began what many have perceived as an accumulation of endless controversies about appropriate music for worship. Keach argued that the neglect of singing was one of the chief causes for "our sad witherings." He argued that singing was the duty of the whole church and not just some select choristers. Clark aims to address the "sad witherings" that remain evident in the evangelical world of the 21st Century.

Much of the music in the Baptist and evangelical worlds of the 20th Century reflected the revivalistic spirit of the time and the words tended to define the drama of salvation more in terms of human response than divine initiative. The gospel music was experientially focused, causing some to reflect that congregational singing was more anthropocentric than theocentric. Clark helps us understand both the horizontal and vertical dimensions of music in our worship. We are called to sing psalms, hymns, and spiritual songs to one another (Eph. 5:19) as well as to worship the Lord with gladness, coming before him with joyful songs (Ps. 100:2).

The Bible makes clear that God desires our praise through music. Music touches us at the emotional and spiritual level in a way rarely paralleled in this life. Music is not only tied to our emotions but also to our memory. For some reason we generally remember more easily what is sung than what is said. Music thus enables us to express praise and worthiness to God because we don't have to struggle to know what to say. We have learned that "Jesus Loves Me This I Know" and thus we "Praise God from Whom All Blessings Flow."

Clark guides us toward renewal in worship by helping us rediscover the missing jewel of worship. In this volume we are invited to recognize the worship of God as a primary function of the church. We are invited to learn that worship is not passive, but active. Clark helps us learn to emphasize that worship is primarily spiritual and symbolic and the Spirit of God enables our singing, prompting our love and praise of God. Clark invites us to think anew about worship in general, but the place of music in worship in particular. He stresses the need for preparation on behalf of believers, both participants and leaders. Finally, we are reminded of the importance of the congregation, strengthening our understanding of the local church. The fresh perspective that we are offered in this book will certainly help us recover the significance of a sense of community and the importance of the local church in the Christian life.

I believe that Clark's book will help restore genuine worship in our lives individually in the lives of our churches. Not only will the body of Christ be enhanced and built up, but the mission and outreach of the church will be strengthened. The people of God who have worshipped their God and who have been mutually strengthened and prepared to enter the world to touch lives, meet needs, counsel hurts, speak to injustices, and by life and witness proclaim the saving message of the Gospel. I am grateful to Paul Clark for his extraordinary contribution to the life of the churches through this fine work. My prayer is that others, after reading this work, will move from their "sad witherings" and join me in singing with great joy:

Praise the Lord, Praise the Lord,
Let the Earth hear His voice.
Praise the Lord, Praise the Lord,
Let the people rejoice.

David S. Dockery, President
Union University,
Jackson, Tennessee

Prelude

This book is for Christians who have a desire to see worship renewed in their own hearts, in their churches, and among Christians everywhere by the Holy Spirit of God. The specific area of address in the book is worship singing, and consideration of the theology and dynamics of worship singing as a contributor to worship renewal. It is written with pastors, worship music leaders, and other church leaders in mind, though I would hope its message would be understandable for those who have ever participated in worship through singing and have curiosity to think seriously about what is taking place when people sing together words of worship. The writing began with a focus devoted almost exclusively to congregational singing. The further I journeyed through this exercise, however, the more I recognized the power and potential of worship singing to aid worship in all of its practiced environments. Since my earliest remembrances I have had a sense that something unique takes place when people sing together. Many people take a level of inspiration from singing a school *alma mater* or joining in the national anthem. When singing is, in fact, worship, however, the unique nature of the practice is taken to an entirely new level of engagement with recognition that the Lord is among us.

A good part of my life has been spent considering the words and music of song. My study and spiritual contemplation of recent years has become enthralled with what happens when these things come together—words, music, and singing people. It is important to note here that I am a Southern Baptist, and that the reflection in this book comes from the tradition and perspective of that faith. There is no doubt that my upbringing influenced my faith life and worldview, including the views related to worship singing and music. At the same time, I admit that recent years have brought about a rich broadening of appreciation of faith traditions other than my own, and the worship *ethos* that is associated with those traditions. I have found this exposure to have strengthened my conviction and sense of confessional relationship within my own Baptist tradition, while at once building a stronger sense of connection to the Church of our Lord Jesus Christ in its many expressions.

Early years of my life were accompanied by sounds of the piano in our home being played by those who had varying levels of talent and training. My mother taught piano lessons in our home nearly every day of the week. When students were playing, the sounds were sometimes laboriously absent of musicality. When my mother or sister was practicing, whether for Sunday church responsibility or for their own enjoyment, the sound seemed to beckon to some sensitivity in me that felt the music and wondered about the feelings. Opportunities to gather around the piano and join the family in singing were meaningful as I became more aware of their rarity and began to gain some sense of what the music we were singing actually meant. Faith and singing have found ways of intermingling as intertwining threads throughout my life. It would be difficult to determine in different phases of life which was leading the way, the faith or the singing. At times it would seem that singing was a determining means of discovering faith origins for me. At other times, the drive of faith demanded a response through confident singing. In each instance, however, I confess that there has been a congregation, a church with which to sing. In formative years, I found immense privilege in joining the song of the church and in growing in my understanding of its meaning and significance. In later years, as one called out to lead, I found some of life's greatest fulfillment in calling the church to join the singing of eternal praise. In retrospect, I am realizing that the singing was only truly meaningful as the Holy Spirit of God was present in the worship, warming hearts, instigating the song, purifying intentions, and singing with us "in the midst of the congregation" (Heb 2:11–13).

The book is organized into substantive areas of consideration in purposeful order. The first chapter invites consideration as to why our worship singing may be in need of a tune-up. It seeks to place the activity of singing into the larger issue, worship. Distinction is drawn between anthropocentric worship (human-centered) and theocentric worship (God-centered). A brief explanation is given as to the importance and difference in content, form, and style of worship. The second chapter of the book is a biblical theology of congregational singing offered through a look at Scriptures that offer examples, models, attitudes, or instructions for singing worship. The chapter also offers an abbreviated historic glimpse of the practice of singing in church worship with a special emphasis on Baptist worship. Chapter three is a view of different kinds of worship gatherings, or groupings for gathered worship, and an appeal to understand worship singing within a given contextual gathering. Chapter four invites the consideration of the words of worship singing. Chapter five naturally follows with consideration of the music of worship singing and a teaser as to how music's own meaning speaks within our worship. Chapter six may seem out of place in a book about singing worship, but the essay that considers Sunday as the preferred day of Christian worship is intended to refocus evangelical church practice to revere the Lord's Day as the day of resurrection celebration and to consider once again elevating the importance of gathering believers to engage in worship on this special day, which includes, of course, the activity of congregational singing. Chapter seven further considers the sacred actions of worship, including the four folds of worship structure: gathering, Word, Table, and sending. Additional attention is given to the ordinances of baptism and the Lord's Supper, as well as dedications and special services of churches. In each instance, thought is directed toward how congregational singing might address these worship actions within liturgy. Chapter eight is a practical section offering points of evidence that worship renewal is either needed or is taking place. It also addresses practical means for applying worship singing to worship actions that may serve the purpose of renewal. Chapter nine is a polemic for conducting a congregational rehearsal for worship singing, and also provides practical suggestions for how such an event might be conducted. Chapter ten utilizes the text of the hymn, "Come, Thou Fount," to outline a call to yield our worship attitudes, spirits, songs, and singing to be tuned by the Holy Spirit of God to serve His purposes in worship.

As one who consults with churches in matters of worship and singing, I find the healthiest church environments to be those in which the preaching pastor and worship music leader are on the same page. In some instances, those persons plan worship together week in and week out. In other instances, those persons simply spend sufficient time ministering together that they trust one another and seem to know each other's hearts, such that their separate planning is woven together as the Spirit guides, given their common thread of understanding. The resultant worship structure is effective in either instance. I am thoroughly convinced of the need for preaching pastors and worship music leaders to spend time together, conversing often about the theological foundations of worship, and considering closely the context in which they serve. It is my fervent prayer that the material of this volume will somehow serve as a resource to foster such conversation between senior pastor and musician. I could hope that pastors would be more intentional in addressing worship singing through their preaching as a result of this book. I would pray that the book would instruct worship music leaders to diligently serve their congregation by encouraging its singing, ever calling attention to the voices of worship, the voice of the Lord revealed through Word, song, and symbol, and the voice of the congregation in making its response through meaningful singing.

Soli Deo Gloria!

Paul B. Clark, Jr.

Acknowledgments

For the most part, making music has seemed to come easy for me most of my life. Writing a book, even one that is focused on the subject that has consumed the greater part of my life, is quite another matter. I give thanks to the Lord for the grace gifts that are the people who have shared the journey of life and song with me. I could never have gone to seminary, then twenty plus years later, gone back to engage in more in-depth worship study without the loving support and partnership of my wife, Ebbie, who has been by my side through every endeavor of life. During days of failing health and subsequent recovery, I was awakened once again to just how blessed I am with two great sons, a great daughter, two daughters-in-law, and a son-in law-to-be. I found much motivation to mind doctors' orders through thoughts of a promising future filled with love and family because of the consistent encouragement of my kids, along with the vision of my two beautiful grandchildren who brighten any room with their presence. The music of the church has always been at home in our house. I am grateful to my parents, brother, and sisters for joining that song at every opportunity and helping establish such a pattern for me to follow and offer to my own home's atmosphere.

I would be remiss not to thank Dr. Frank Lewis, the Sanctuary Choir, and music ministry staff of the First Baptist Church of Nashville, Tennessee, who supported me through doctoral projects that allowed research within that historic church where rich congregational singing is a familiar strain of vibrant worship. I want to thank Rev. Wayne Causey, Minister of Music and Worship at Forest Hills Baptist Church, for his friendship and support of projects related to worship studies. Dr. Jonathan Nelms, Rev. Mark Edwards, and others have offered patient support reading and responding to portions of this work. Their friendship and professional insight are treasured gifts.

I want to thank pastors, seminary professors, colleagues, and friends across thirty-five years of ministry who have been mentors, models, and partners and have helped engrave the song into my heart, and helped me know the joy of its singing. I want to thank my music ministers who demonstrated ways for me that I later emulated as I practiced the pairing of what I knew of pastoring, learned mostly from observing my father, and what I knew of music as ministry, most of which I learned from those music ministers. I especially want to thank Dr. Jim Hart and the faculty and community of the Robert E. Webber Institute for Worship Studies for the wealth of information, the introduction to historic, as well as new forms of liturgical expression, for the spirit of humility and inclusion that characterizes the IWS community, and the passion for learning that was renewed through my days of study through that institution. I especially thank my "Xi" class and David Manner for their shared joy in learning.

Chapter 1

NEEDING A WORSHIP TUNE-UP

When I was fourteen, I received my first guitar as a Christmas present. It was not an expensive guitar, but I saw it as the key to my future, as much as a fourteen-year-old boy can ascertain his future while daydreaming about a life filled with music emanating from a box with six strings. I envisioned a future in which when I played this thing, girls would shriek like they did at the sight of the Beatles, and schoolmates would stand in amazement at the power of my music. All I needed was some help in learning chords, some music, and a few years of practice on this instrument that at first felt strange in my hands. I borrowed a Mel Bay starter guitar book from a friend. I jumped right to the pages where it showed how to form chords with your fingers. I looked for what appeared to be the easiest chord to make and tried to press the strings. It wasn't as easy as I expected, but I got them down and strummed all six strings with a good full stroke, for a rookie. And … yuck! Something was totally wrong. I thought, "Is this thing broken?" Perhaps mom and dad could not afford a real guitar, and this Silvertone they placed under the Christmas tree was really just a toy. I tried another strum. Nope, still awful. I tried forming another chord, hoping for better results. Different tones, but still sounded terrible. What was wrong? I flipped to the first pages in the Mel

Bay book and found instruction on tuning the guitar. Aha! This could be the problem.

Carefully, I made my way through the tuning process one string at a time, of course. As I found the matching pitch for each string and then tried forming the chord again, it gave me hope, as each time it got a little more musical. No matter how excited I was when I first picked up the guitar, there was just not much value in attempts at music-making until I got this instrument tuned.

Tuning my heart to sing God's grace in worship is much more than a metaphor for a thematic study. It is a lifelong engagement that calls for full-life commitment and is itself totally dependent upon the sovereign and powerful God whose name it claims and proposes to exalt. Like the guitar string, the heart cannot be tuned without the application and release of tension. Life is lived in a context of many distractions and conflicting appeals that press us in directions that loosen our proverbial strings away from the pitches intended by the Master. Obviously, the guitar is not a self-tuning instrument. Likewise, it is futile for us to attempt to tune our own hearts to sing the praise of the Lord's grace. A right heart is a necessary ingredient for singing our worship in a manner pleasing to God and in harmony with our fellow believers. Group singing, as is the case in congregational worship, becomes even more complex in that there is not one heart to be tuned, but rather many hearts to be tuned individually and at the same time tuned together like a symphonic orchestra, or like the strings of the guitar. The strings, like the symphony's instruments, depend not only on their own tuning, but the tuning of the whole ensemble to bring the best music to reality. Hearts tuned in worship offer the praise of pure unisons and beautifully blended and balanced harmony of life, faith, and community. In later chapters, we will explore some of these complexities and research the mysterious dynamics and power resonant in gathered worship singing. We will also unpack some of what it means to have our hearts tuned by God. An important aspect of that consideration of how we might be made "in tune" with God is our first consideration of what it might mean to worship Him. What does it mean to place our churches and our lives in a position to be humbled, forgiven, and renewed through an ongoing "spiritual tune-up?"

Everybody Worships and Everything is Worship

Worshiping is not unique to Christians. There is a sense in which everybody worships. Harold Best says that "nobody does not worship. ... for as long as this world endures, everybody inhabiting it is bowing down and serving something or someone."[1] Christians sometimes forget that it is quite possible for that "something or someone to be other than Jesus." A. W. Tozer further reminds us that "authentic worship is altogether possible apart from Christ."[2] The question is not whether or not we worship, but rather what or who we worship. In the case of Christian worship, the question is also how we are engaged in that worship. Christian worship is unique in that the One we worship is engaged with us in the worship. In fact, as we will see, Christian worship is not possible without His involvement. He is not just receiving the worship, but is communing with us in His three-person reality.

Worship is probably what we are seeing on an October afternoon in East Tennessee when automobiles are lined up on I-40 for fifteen miles from the heart of downtown Knoxville. People adorned in orange and white trudging through congested traffic to attend the "ceremony of the pigskin" are participating in important aspects of the ritual. Tradition is important at Pigskin Community Church. The processional begins with a sixty-year tradition reverently called "the Vol walk," in which gladiators descend from the room of preparation to the stadium of battle, cheered on by adoring fans, all accompanied by a familiar strain of song that joins three or four generations in shared singing. Tennessee football is an object of worship for those in the "Vol Nation" of "Big Orange Country." The same could be said of fans of collegiate or professional sports of all kinds in cities and states all across our country and, indeed, in locations all around the world.

The *who* or *what* that becomes the object of worship can be a deity, a celebrity, a political figure, or a bonafide hero. Worship can be invested in some human attribute, such as power, fame, or wealth. We can even worship ourselves. The object of our worship is usually obvious. In fact, the title of G. K. Beale's book states it well: *We Become What We Worship.*[3] His

1 Harold Best, *Unceasing Worship: Biblical Perspectives on Worship and the Arts* (Downers Grove, IL: InterVarsity Press, 2003), 17.

2 A. W. Tozer, *Whatever Happened to Worship? A Call to True Worship* (Camp Hill, PA: Christian Publications, 1985), 38.

3 G. K. Beale, *We Become What We Worship: A Biblical Theology of Idolatry* (Downers Grove, ILInterVarsity Press, 2008).

volume is a work on idolatry. Though the book you are presently reading is primarily concerned with the singing of worship, we must first establish just who or what it is we are worshiping before we can assess the dynamics of the singing or the appropriateness of the songs being sung to express that worship. Renewal calls us to test the spirits that drive our present practice. Recent reformation within my own denomination resulted in more robust affinity to biblical orthodoxy in educational and publishing environments, yet other than the focus of preaching, remained strangely silent toward what is arguably the most effective center of Christian practice and most formative center of what we understand of God: corporate worship. Baptist theologian, W. T. Conner calls worship "the first business of the church."[4]

Sadly, the recent "resurgence" in Southern Baptist life did not include attention to worship singing. If we are honest, we will likely perceive that worship singing in many Baptist and other evangelical churches has continued a self-absorbed path that lifts and celebrates our worship more than it does the Trinitarian God that it claims to be its subject and object. The "people of the book" we claim to be seem infatuated more by the hunger for charismatic speakers who talk *about* the Scripture than they seem concerned at the remarkably scant opportunities whereby the Scripture is read aloud as a centerpiece of public worship practice in their own churches.

Perhaps our best clue as to what we are worshiping is a close examination of what we are becoming. Examples from Old and New Testaments demonstrate this very notion as we find people worshiping dead idols only to lose their own life. The activity and cultic practice of worship has become such a focus in contemporary church that it is certainly possible that persons and churches begin to worship worship itself. Such worship is little, if at all, more than worshiping self, seeking self-gratification through experience. I recall hearing Dr. Don Hustad refer to such persons as "inspiration junkies." So the question I would raise in relation to the practice of Christian worship in many of our churches would be whether worship's ethos within these expressions has moved from a theocentric (God-centered) practice to an anthropocentric (human-centered) one, where the subject and/or object of worship has become the experience of the humans involved in it. As such, this worship could metaphorically be "out of tune."

4 W. T. Conner, *The Gospel of Redemption* (Nashville: Broadman, 1943), 276.

One question that arises in response to this postulation is how can we know? What are determining factors that indicate an act or environment has drifted across some imaginary line and now finds the controlling point of its practice to be centered in what gives pleasure to the human(s) participating in the practice? Note that this is not to say that in theocentric worship human participants never receive pleasure. To the contrary, the Westminster Catechism states, "The chief end of man is to glorify God and to enjoy Him forever." In the God-human relationship, the notion of enjoyment and the piety of spirited adulation are woven into the fabric of the relationship itself and indeed seem to carry something of the connotation of the meaning of what it is to worship. However, though the line of demarcation is evasive, mysterious, and quite likely impossible to clearly define, it is only reasonable to postulate that there is a point at which worship, even so-called Christian worship, is no longer genuinely God-centered, but rather has become a kind of idolatry that could be called idiosyncratic, anthropocentric, or, even "worshiping idolatrously."[5]

Though I take into account the limitation of my own position as being within the story that I attempt to describe and as such, avoid declaration of a naïvely presumed objectivity, still I believe it is incumbent on me and all worship leadership to identify practices, nuance, and attitude reflection that would signify that the controlling point of worship may have shifted from a theocentric to an anthropocentric motivation.

A popular statement among evangelical worship leadership these days is, it's not about you, or, it's not about me. The posit sounds correct, and often meets with affirming response by would-be worshipers. The inference, of course, is that worship is about God. Theological rigor would likely stand in that corner, as would most ecclesiastical authority. Careful attention, however, to what can be observed in the means of expression in much of today's corporate worship may indicate a different motivational center. Patterns of communal worship attendance in many local churches demonstrate a weak commitment and understanding of what it is to be the church. Consumeristic means of church selection, worship promotion, and even worship planning are often further indicators of worship motivated by what we think may please people. The struggle with the controlling point for Christian worship appears to be trapped in the same human condition that detracts believers from faithful discipleship, persistent mission engagement, unconditional *koinonia,* and genuine servanthood.

5 Best, *Unceasing Worship,* 164. Best is describing golden calflike attempts to reduce God to substance rather than faith.

In each of these instances, our struggle to gain control ends up serving to render us very much out of control, and metaphorically out of tune. It would appear that any movement toward renewing our worship would involve moving in the direction of subjecting ourselves, bowing down, humbling ourselves before the Lord, acknowledging our complete inability to tune ourselves, and seeking renewal from Christian worship's only possible power source, the Holy Spirit. The Calvin Institute of Worship aptly reminds us that "worship renewal is not something that human ingenuity or creativity can produce," and indeed that it "is a gift of God's Spirit for which we pray, rather than an accomplishment we achieve."[6]

I contend that an application of congregational singing to assist in the engagement of the congregation in communal worship can serve the purpose of worship renewal for reasons that will be further explored in this work. Humbling ourselves and subjecting ourselves as considered here calls for a spirit that is contrary to the kind of power-seeking and institutional positioning we often see in the market-driven environment of today's church. It runs in stark contrast to the self-serving models that have become absorbed in issues of cultural appeal. Following this path has led many churches to seek the most popular and presumed people-drawing styles of music, which is by definition anthropocentric. Focus on music styles for worship has divided the evangelical community. Addressing this issue within Baptist life, statesman David Dockery notes well, "For Baptists to move forward toward renewal in our worship will require time, patience, and careful instruction. Learning from the strengths of each style can enhance our celebration and produce a more mature, balanced worship." He goes further to state, "we must help people learn that worship is not passive but active. We gather on the Lord's Day not so much to receive, but to offer sacrifices of praise (see Heb 13:15–16). We acknowledge what God has done for us and is doing for us."[7]

The truth is that, in our humanity, especially in postmodern culture, we are rendered helpless against the disabling urgency of *me*, having my own needs met. We live in a culture of *self* with emphasis on self-gratification, self-reliance, self-actualization, and self-empowerment, all achieved through so-called self-help. To turn the focus of Christian worship toward an emphasis that would purposely appeal to selves in

---

6 Calvin Institute of Worship, *What Is Worship Renewal?* www.calvin.edu/worship/wshp_renewal.php (accessed 17 August 2007).

7 David S. Dockery, *Southern Baptist Consensus and Renewal* (Nashville: B&H, 2008), 124–125.

the supposed interest of evangelizing runs a high risk of losing a genuine God-centeredness as the controlling point of worship. Our cultic practice in Christian worship, though bearing the name of Christ, is often hijacked by this tyrannical urgency. Our heart is stolen by our need to be inspired and entertained. We are confused by a sense of emotional entitlement that our culture has taught us to expect in return for investing our time, money, and vulnerability. Scripture teaches us, "For where your treasure is, there your heart will be also" (Matt 6:21).

The music of worship, and congregational singing in particular, would seem to hold potential as a means of ascertaining the grip of renewal in Christian worship.

Definitions of Worship

Most any study of worship practice or theology posits a working definition. A difficulty in defining Christian worship is that no one word for worship is translated from Hebrew or Greek to English. Rather, there are gestures, words, attitudes, and actions that reflect what we have come to call "worship" that are translated "worship." Even worse, writers who simply use the English word "worship," tracing its etymology from *weorthscipe*, with its connotation of "ascribing worth," leave us open to the subtle but destructive practice of assuming that we stand in a position to determine God's worth.[8] This presumption seems in itself anthropocentric.

Theocentric Worship

Theologian David Peterson's hypothesis states that "… the worship of the living and true God is essentially *an engagement with him on the terms that he proposes and in the way that he alone makes possible.*"[9] The dialogical pattern set forth in Scripture is a developing interchange, but the provision is in each instance determined by God's work, God's actions, and God's grace. It is true that worship involves or engages the human will to act in response in a manner that pays tribute, honors, recognizes, and affirms worth, but for worship to remain theocentric, it would seem it must continuously recognize the provisional nature and dependency upon the "wholly other, "holy other" that we worship. That is to say that theocentric

8 Peterson, *Engaging with God,* 17. Peterson is referencing W. Eichrodt, *Theology of the Old Testament* (ET, London: SCM, 1961; Philadelphia: Westminster, 1967), Vol. 1, p. 102.

9 Ibid., 20.

worship at every point recognizes the godliness of God, as in the ancient church prayer hymn, "Te Deum," which in essence proclaims, God, You are God, which also implies, I am not. The idea of *engagement* in Peterson's hypothesis implies the active participation of both beings, but perspective is more fully realized with the rest of the statement that demonstrates that initiation and means come from God. Any provision to humankind is a provision of grace. The greatest Gift to us is Jesus Christ, God incarnate, "the Lamb of God who takes away the sin of the world." Jesus' conversation with the Samaritan woman at Sycar gives understanding that He is the "living water." God is active in the provision of worship. The Father, Whom we worship, is seeking worshipers who will worship Him "in spirit and truth" (John 4:21–24). A biblical theology of worship makes this clear and its ultimate model can be stated, This was Jesus' worship, to do the will of the Father.[10] This further illustrates and heightens the mystery that is Christian worship, and intensifies the implication that appropriate response in the dialogue is available because of God, directed toward God, and on God's terms.

Anthropocentric Worship

If Marva Dawn's summation is correct, whereby, in genuine theocentric worship, God is both the subject and object of worship, it seems logical that any shift toward man, and most especially an individual self, becoming one or the other of those (subject or object) is indication that worship has become anthropocentric. Relating this notion to Peterson's hypothesis, we could say that in anthropocentric worship practice the "engagement with God" has begun to be on man's terms, rather than the "terms He (God) proposes," or that it has taken an expression other than one that "He alone can provide." Emotive means of attempted engagement can shift to become self-absorbed, self-actualizing, and the intention itself may become self-fulfilling. Dawn says the controlling tension is between "meaning systems," one of which is "inductive," and the other of which is "deductive." The former centers on attempts to achieve "wholeness," in life's experiences; the latter on belief in God. In theistic worship, "God not only influences daily life, but also shapes all of reality and makes life meaningful in some ultimate sense." Indeed, we "who live by the name

10 Andrew Hill, in a response post on "Xi's class message board for the Robert E. Webber Institute for Worship Studies" dated February 21, 2006 at 20:51:43.

Christian are those rescued from ourselves by the salvation wrought by Jesus."[11]

"Because we are finite, we will inevitably worship something or someone."[12] Anthropocentric worship, then, begins to develop the god it wants to see, or more directly the god the worshiper wants to see and thus becomes the control of subject and object of worship. "We can represent Jesus to suit us, whether as an early version of Trotsky or as a beach-boy guru or as the archetypical social worker or as whatever turns us on, while claiming at the same time to remain perfectly orthodox and biblical in our thinking about the Son."[13] Since it is the "me" we are seeking to please at whatever level of conscious effort in this scenario, this points to self-love. D. A. Carson says, "At the heart of the Fall is the self-love that destroys our God-centeredness. Implicitly, of course, all failure to worship God is neither more nor less than idolatry." Harold Best unveils the process in his statement, "Idolatry is the act of shaping something that we then allow to shape us. We craft our own destiny and then act as if it were supernaturally revealed."[14]

Everybody worships, and what's more, everything is worship. Any human action has some motivation, however basic or complex. There is nothing that we do that does not stem from our gaze toward someone, or something, some objective. It is how we were made. We were made to worship. Actually, that is an incomplete statement for those who claim Christian faith. The biblical teaching is that God's children have been made to worship God. The apostle Paul compels us with a sense of urgency, "I beg you ('I appeal to you' HCSB) brothers, by the mercies of God to offer your bodies as a living sacrifice, holy and acceptable unto God for this is your reasonable act of worship" (Rom 12:1). Offering our bodies in this instance indicates our whole selves. As we think of worship, whether personal or in community, we are to bring our whole selves to worship the true and living God. All of our desires, needs, frailty, every aspect of our personality and total being is to be offered up as living sacrifice. It is only "reasonable" that this should be so. Our total being, mind, body, soul,

---

11 Dawn, Marva. *Reaching Out without Dumbing Down: A Theology of Worship for the Turn-of-the-Century Culture* (Grand Rapids: Eerdmans, 1995), 76, 82–86.

12 Carson, D. A. *Worship by the Book* (Grand Rapids: Zondervan, 2002), 34.

13 Robert Jenson. "With No Qualifications: The Christological Maximalism of the Christian East," in *Ancient and Postmodern Christianity: Paleo-Orthodoxy in the 21st Century,* Kenneth Tanner and Christopher A. Hall, ed. (Downers Grove, IL: InterVarsity Press, 2002), 19.

14 Best, *Unceasing Worship,* 163.

and strength are to be offered to God, nothing held back. Everything is worship. It is the first and most important commandment according to Jesus.

> Jesus replied: "Love the Lord your God with all your heart and with all your soul and with all your mind." This is the first and greatest commandment. And the second is like it: "Love your neighbor as yourself" (Matt 22:37–39).

David Peterson reminds us that the reverence and fear of the Lord found in the Old Testament were obedience to all the covenant demands of God. While these attitudes were certainly present in cultic activity in the temple, tabernacle, or synagogue, the "reference was normally to the honoring of God by total lifestyle."[15] Homage, service, reverence, and praise are aspects of the whole of life. This certainly reflects a bigger picture than contemporary Christians have often portrayed, implying that worship is summed up either in a quiet attitude in church attendance, or through an emotive, spirited, overt display of enthusiasm in praise.

Where worship singing is concerned, the value of offering ourselves as a "living" sacrifice should be obvious. The physical act of singing calls for beings that are alive with blood flowing through veins and vocal chords capable of vibrating in response to the grace gift given so freely through the ultimate sacrifice of the perfect One who died for us. The Romans passage goes on to discuss this grace.

> For by the grace given to me I say to everyone among you not to think of himself more highly than he ought to think, but to think with sober judgment, each according to the measure of faith that God has assigned. For as in one body we have many members, and the members do not all have the same function, so we, though many, are one body in Christ, and individually members one of another (Rom 12:3–8).

Two great themes of Christian worship emanate from this passage. One theme is the spirit of genuine humility. An honest perception of ourselves in relation to who God is would seem to move us toward the worshipful attitude to which the New Testament seems to clearly point. The humble spirit that results from seeing the Lord "high and lifted up" (Isaiah 6) has a way of placing all of our relationships in order. In the Romans passage

---

15 David Peterson, *Engaging with God*, 73.

we are reminded "not to think of ourselves more highly than we ought to think," which seems to make our relation to God Himself our plumb line to determine how we see others around us. This profound truth is certainly not an easy one in a culture teeming with messages that cry for us to see ourselves as better than others.

The other theme addressed in the Roman passage is another consistent theme of Christian faith and worship, that of unity. Christ prayed that his disciples would be one, even in the same way that he, Jesus, and the Father were one. The attitude needed for worship singing is the kind of humility reflected in this passage. As we examine the idea that everybody worships and everything is worship, we must ask ourselves if our shaping of worship and worship singing adheres to the admonition to "not think of yourself more highly than you ought." Humility can be a challenging attribute to lay upon the altar for the worship-leading musician whose talents are notably superior to the congregation singers he or she is called upon to lead. We will spend more time unpacking what it means to lead congregational worship singing pastorally in a later chapter. I mention this attitude of humility now as it must be understood as an irreducible minimum when giving any serious consideration to the worship of God. The spirit of humbleness is an absolute prerequisite to any worship action that would be acceptable to a holy God. Isaiah 6:1–8 serves as one of the most-oft referenced passages in relation to our worship. It clearly describes the attitude of humility, woe is me, as the spirit of approach to the subject and object of worship, namely the Lord who is "high and lifted up," and in whose presence Isaiah ultimately responded, "here am I, send me" (Isa 6:8).

With this backdrop in mind, I want to invite your consideration to the worship of the congregation, and specifically to congregational singing as a means of aiding worship renewal. Given our disclaimer of the only means of true renewal to be the work of the Holy Spirit, I ask you to pray that even your reading of this material would be guided by Him, and that any actions toward which you might be drawn for your own life or for your exercise of leadership would first be tested against the pages of Holy Scripture.

Substance, Form, and Style of Worship

The so-called worship wars of recent years have centered almost exclusively in questions about style. My own experience in church consultations has been saturated with helping pastors, musicians, and lay leaders determine adjustments needed to accommodate members of the congregation who demonstrate preferences for diverse styles of music, variety in atmosphere, or who are looking to reach out to their communities through updated styles in their worship expression.

Robert Webber and others remind us that the first question of worship is not about style at all, but rather must be concerned with the substance or content of worship. What is worship ultimately about? Who is the worship for? Who are we trying to please in worship? What is the source of the power of worship? What will be the content of our worship? These are questions that point us toward the true substance of worship. Some leaders presume the question of substance is a given, but a little evaluation and conversation with church members often demonstrates a different story. I consulted in one church where one of the deacons of the church, when asked who worship was really about, responded by accusing the pastor, worship leader, and this consultant of being facetious for asking such a question. His follow-up statements displayed that we should know that worship is "about the people, of course." Before any other steps can be taken toward worship renewal, we need to be certain that, to the extent it is possible for us, we understand the substance of worship. Such understanding is rooted in and tested by biblical truth, constantly subjected to theological scrutiny, informed by historic practice, and informed by contemporary context, and relentlessly bathed in prayer for Holy Spirit illumination.

Another aspect of worship that is less critical, but highly important, is the form or structure of worship. We cannot really evaluate the stylistic approach to worship until we understand the form into which that style is to fit. Form helps us understand how we will approach the God we worship. The form of our worship brings the congregation together in a common journey we share with one another and with others in the larger church of all the saints. Those of us who are of the free-church tradition may recoil at the suggestion of a set form, preferring instead to be led by the Spirit. A little study, however, will likely show us that the liturgy of the free church has a clear, repeated pattern in its worship practice. Our need is likely not so much to recreate a form, but rather to be sure we understand and follow the form we use with purpose and direction in our worship, and more importantly to subject the form to biblical inspection.

The last question of worship is the style. The style of worship has much to do with who is gathering, common means of artistic expression, and shared understandings of the culture in which the worshipers live. Robert Webber states that "style is not now, nor has it ever been, a matter of biblical tradition."[16] This is not to imply that style does not need to reflect the spirit of the Gospel, or of the worship. Rather, it is a recognition that style is a point of communication, bringing forward the question of relevance within the cultural context for the worshipers gathering. Determining style helps the leaders to plan the language and music for worship that will help worshipers follow the form as they engage in the substance of authentic Christian worship.

Prioritizing these considerations will assist in selection of congregational songs, accompaniment textures, and timbre of worship leadership for singing, as leadership contemplates the revelation of the triune God in appropriate reference to His character and doctrine. Such prioritization exercised with prayerful sensitivity will surely reflect God's grace, and lay the groundwork for inviting and encouraging worshipers to join the song by adding their heart and voice to the singing. Misunderstanding the order of these considerations is often the culprit that draws leaders to wrong conclusions and premature actions in trying to bring about change in their congregations. The primary offender is a drive to present a stylistic atmosphere that will draw persons to attend worship in the specific church. The wrong thinking drives leaders to allow the controlling point of worship to become the style. Form may begin to be unclear if not even intentionally scrambled as a strategy to keep people on their toes, so they will not know what is coming next in worship. Worse yet, the content of worship may lose its preeminence in these settings, confusing the priority of staying fresh (style) with trusting the Gospel (substance) to be the true power of the message in worship.

I am offering the thoughts and reflections contained in the pages to follow as fodder for contemplation by pastors, worship music leaders, church and denominational leaders, and all Christians concerned with worship practices of today's church. My focus is worship singing, though I recognize such activity is practiced within the larger framework that is Christian worship. I encourage you to read with a prayer that your reading might open new ways to understand worship singing, and give fresh insight to renew your spirit, and thereby renew your song. Such renewal can only occur by the power and presence of the Holy Spirit.

---

16 Robert Webber, *Planning Blended Worship: The Creative Mixture of Old & New* (Nashville: Abingdon Press, 1998), 22.

Chapter 2

BIBLICAL, THEOLOGICAL, AND HISTORICAL FOUNDATIONS FOR SINGING WORSHIP

Where were you when I laid the earth's foundation?
Tell me, if you understand.

Who marked off its dimensions? Surely you know!
Who stretched a measuring line across it?

On what were its footings set,
or who laid its cornerstone—
while the morning stars sang together
and all the angels shouted for joy? (Job 38:4–7) [1]

In order to develop a deeper understanding of congregational singing dynamics in corporate worship, and to foster an intentional focus on engaging more of the congregation in active participation in worship through singing, we must first establish a biblical, historical, and theological foundation for such an emphasis. In this chapter, I want to engage in theological reflection on congregational singing. It is important to study selected biblical passages that offer examples and instruction for

1 All biblical references are taken from the Holy Bible, New International Version.

singing our worship, and glean from them possible application for our worship. In addition to this biblical reflection, I want to briefly describe the historical development of singing in worship including a historical focus on Baptists.

Theological Starting Point

Deepening one's understanding of congregational singing in corporate worship begins with theological reflection. "Where theologians begin, influences where their theological reflections will lead them."[2] Gregory Thornbury states, "Christian theology advances the bold assertion that truth, goodness, and beauty cannot be known apart from God, their author," and furthermore that "it is impossible to know the creature apart from the Creator."[3] A central reality of the human condition for believers is found in our confession, "We have not loved you as we ought," or "We have not loved you with our whole heart and mind and strength." Nor have we "loved our neighbor as we ought."[4] To reflect theologically on congregational singing in worship means I must keep the larger context of worship in view, and that view not in a vacuum of my own control or presumed objectivity; rather, I must wrestle and succumb at every point to the truth of the biblical narrative and return full attention to the one to and for whom "the morning stars sang together and all the angels shouted for joy" (Job 38:7).

My starting point is perhaps best articulated through the definition of worship adopted in the last chapter, that of David K. Peterson, who states, "The worship of the living and true God is essentially an engagement with him on the terms that he proposes and in the way that he alone makes possible."[5] Such dependency further illustrates and heightens the mystery that is Christian worship, and intensifies the implication that appropriate response in the dialogue is available because of God, directed toward God, and on God's terms. We recognize the only possibility of our access

---

2 Howard W. Stone and James O. Duke, *How to Think Theologically* (Minneapolis: Fortress Press, 2006), 60.

3 Gregory Alan Thornbury, "Prolegomena: Introduction to the Task of Theology" in *A Theology for the Church* ed. Daniel L. Akin (Nashville: Broadman & Holman Academics, 2007), 2–3.

4 *The Worship Sourcebook* (Grand Rapids, MI: Baker Books, 2004), 89. Traditional prayer of confession found in the *Book of Common Prayer,* as well as many other worship guides.

5 David K. Peterson, *Engaging with God: A Biblical and Theological Foundation for Worship* (Downers Grove, IL: InterVarsity Press, 1992), 20.

as coming from God through the work of Christ, drawn by the Spirit. Participation in worship, as all activities of Christian faith, needs full integration with the doctrine of the Trinity. "God's beauty is the actual living exchange between Father, Son, and Holy Spirit, as this exchange is perfect simply as exchange, as it *sings* ... Correspondingly, our enjoyment of God is that we are taken into the triune singing. Perhaps we may say that we are allowed to double the parts."[6]

As we look to the biblical record for reflection on singing in worship, we do so with the foundational understanding that its subject and object is God, as is the case with all of true Christian worship. Marva Dawn reminds us of the foundational truth, "Worship is *for* God" (italics mine).[7] As we will see in our examples, singing often participates in revealing and re-revealing the reasons for the very praise it also seeks to express. The singing that lauds the Lord it praises also participates in His revelation. In the same vein, theological and historical reflection concerning dynamics of congregational singing in worship would seem to serve the purpose of worship renewal.

Biblical Foundations for Singing as Worship

Job 38:7

The book of Job makes reference to "morning stars" singing together as God acts to create the earth. Commentators indicate that the "morning stars" in this text could refer to heavenly beings other than angels, may be a redundant referral to angels themselves, or might even reference the spirit of all creation at the time of the earth's inception. In any case, it seems clear that contained within this message to Job in God's self-revelation to him is a notion that the song and the singing of praise pre-date the very foundation of the earth.

In the Lord's rhetorical question to Job, "where were you ... when the morning stars sang together?" sound is presupposed. Studies outside the theological discipline have given serious consideration to the place of sound within the context of the universe. Pythagoras' discovery of intervallic relationship and consonant harmony in sixth century BCE led him to theorize that "the harmony of the universe can be expressed in

6 Robert Jenson, *Systematic Theology, Vol I* (Oxford University Press, 1997), 235–236.

7 Marva Dawn, *How Shall We Worship? Biblical Guidelines for the Worship Wars* (Carol Stream, IL: Tyndale House, 2003), 21.

mathematical ratios or proportions apprehended by the mind and musical sounds can mediate these ratios." His line of thinking continued with a notion of the "music of the spheres"—the belief that planets and stars of different sizes emit different pitches, generating a huge, though inaudible to the human ear, cosmic music.[8] Symphonic musical compositions have been based on a variety of sources discovered to be singing along in the created order. Interesting notions of vibratory tones made with regular pattern by the spinning planets and stars, communicative tones of porpoises and whales, and the oft-mentioned song of the bird have been basis for exploration by philosophers, scientists, and religious thinkers of most faith systems.

While not all who address the song do so from a Christian viewpoint, "the song" seems present just the same. Jesus reminded the Pharisees that if the disciples' praise was silenced, indeed the rocks would cry out (Luke 19:40). If we trace the music, the song, and the singing of worship through the whole of history, we find that it is ever present, even into eternity.

From Job 38:7 we can glean that singing as worship occurs in the presence of God and his activity; that singing as worship pre-dates humanity and is in a sense written into the very essence of the universe and therefore, our singing joins a continuum of song that will not be silenced. The passage from Job clearly places the singing of God's praise as part of the grand design of God's complete creation. As such, singing our worship transcends manmade value systems, such as that which seeks to qualify it as good or bad music, or that which would seek to use it to attract people by its own appeal. From Job we see that the highest value of singing is built in to the very structure of the universe from "before the earth was formed."

Exodus 15:1–18

The first biblical record of group singing by God's people is found in Exodus 15:1–18. The children of Israel had just experienced the miraculous deliverance by the Lord at the Red Sea. Not only were they delivered from the watery grave that parted to let them pass through on dry ground, but the Lord used the same waters to destroy the enemy behind them. Stanley Grenz writes, "Israel's singing on the day of the Exodus was surely

8 Jeremy S. Begbie, *Resounding Truth: Christian Wisdom in the World of Music* (Grand Rapids, MI: Baker Academic, 2007), 79.

correct, for music is a natural human response to the saving experience."[9] It appears the song of response was composed instantaneously. David Stuart points out, "There is no need to assume—indeed it would be incorrect to assume—that Moses (or anyone else) would have required weeks, months, years, or decades to put together such a song." The song contained ingredients characteristic of most Hebrew hymns. Stuart says these can be summarized by the initials "SRR: summons to praise, reasons to praise, recapitulation."[10]

The song of Moses and the Israelites, as well as Miriam's reprise that follows, not only serves as a song to indicate a response to God's acts, but serves as a response to God himself. In the singing of the song, we may find the revelation of God and the response to Him in worship. Grenz affirms, "Indeed, singing and worship have been integrally connected since God first constituted Israel as his people."[11]

In the face of God's overpowering deliverance, his people sing. The singing does not center on their faith, but rather on Yahweh's provision. Andy Hill states, "The purpose of worship in the Old Testament is the glorification of God, not the commendation of any human faith response. The point of biblical narrative is to praise Yahweh as the faithful provider for his people (Gen 22:14)."[12]

In the Red Sea experience, the Israelites encountered God's action in the physical world. They responded in the physical world through a physical expression of singing. Water that would have drowned the children of Israel was cleared that they might go through on dry ground, breathing oxygen they needed. The air was now set in vibration as the children of Israel resonated their victorious hymn of praise, and all of this singing is in the physical world.

Great theological themes are included without much development in the singing of this "Song of the Sea." These themes include intentional praise, water, majesty of God, awesome works of God, deliverance, security, and the eternal nature of God. The singing of the story with all its theological implications clearly participates in passing on the truths.

---

9 Stanley J. Grenz, *Theology for the Community of God* (Grand Rapids, MI: Eerdmans Publishing, 2000), 492.

10 David K. Stuart, *Exodus* in *The New American Bible Commentary* (Nashville: Broadman & Holman, 2003), 347.

11 Grenz, *Theology for the Community of God,* 492.

12 Andrew E. Hill, *Enter His Courts with Praise: Old Testament Worship for the New Testament Church* (Grand Rapids, MI: Baker Books, 1996), 33.

"One can imagine groups of Israelites singing the song often on their way to Mt. Sinai and during the wilderness wanderings after leaving Sinai, as a new, replacement generation learned some of their history through music."[13] One of the outcomes of singing among the people of God is the passing of the history and hope of Yahweh.

In summary, the passage reminds us that music and singing are natural human responses to the divine activity of God. It demonstrates that the song for worship singing can be composed almost instantaneously, as well as developed within set patterns. The passage shows that singing can participate in revealing God even as it is responding to God in its singing. It reminds us that worship through singing does not focus on our faith, but on God; and that singing the song of deliverance repeatedly helps us remember his acts and passes the truth of God on to future generations. In this passage from Exodus, as in the Job passage, we are reminded that the highest value system to be served by our singing is that which contributes to and thus participates in the praise and worship of our God, our deliverer. This value system is the motivation of theocentric worship, whereas the value systems identified as being active in problem situations is anthropocentric. As we will see through further biblical study, the song of deliverance continues throughout the biblical record, and indeed is included in the description of the eternal song of heaven (Revelation 15:3). The song of deliverance always participates with God. There is no self-help salvation. It is always dependent upon a Savior.

The Psalms

Scholars recognize psalmody as the oldest continuous musical tradition in Western civilization.[14] Any discussion of singing in worship must reflect upon the Psalter to maintain any sense of biblical integrity as these song-poem-prayers have been the core of worship language throughout the history of Christian worship. The fact of their canonization and placement at the Bible's center speaks of the importance of singing faith and worship. There is a sense in which the psalms represent the whole of worship singing. The psalms give rise to the full range of expression for worshipers in both private and gathered settings. They present in clear terms the tensions to be embraced in any honest living in relationship to God, His world,

13 Stuart, *Exodus*, 347.

14 Piero Weiss and Richard Taruskin, *Music in the Western World: A History in Document* (Belmont, CA: Wadsworth Group/Thomson Learning, 1984), 15–24.

and His people, and therefore present tensions to be embraced in our worship as well. Don Saliers points to the Psalms as having "provided powerful juxtapositions of precisely these realities: the suffering, the sense of abandonment, the glory and the praise, the laments and the thanksgivings." Some of the songs are "untouched by praise" (Ps 88), while others "fluctuate wildly between anxiety and hope" (Ps 42).[15] Indeed, "the Psalms draw our entire life under the rule of God, where everything may be submitted to the God of the gospel."[16]

The truth that God speaks through his word expressed in community is fundamental to the meaning and value of congregational singing through all of Christian history. The Psalms draw the community together to hear in community. Walter Brueggemann points out, "In this literature the community of faith has heard and continues to hear the sovereign speech of God, who meets the community in its depths of need and in its heights of celebration."[17] Though words of a particular psalm may carry intensely personal expression, the *singing* of those expressions in corporate gathering conjoins the worshiping body into one. In the case of a lament, for instance, it is not just that fellow worshipers somehow "feel the pain" of one member's hurt expressed in a psalm, but rather that the congregation genuinely laments as one body.

There is a sense in which the psalms represent for worshipers the larger corpus of a kind of singing that expresses spiritual condition, including spiritual change. As such, any worship renewal activity will surely make frequent use of the Psalter so rich in expression of sensitivities to spiritual renewal. Walter Brueggemann organizes the psalms into three groupings: psalms of orientation, psalms of disorientation, and psalms of new orientation. He notes that human life is characteristically located either in the actual experience of one of these groupings, or in movement from one to the other. Psalms of orientation reflect a condition of well-being and what might be called a "right side up" relationship in the order of things.[18] When the singing congregation rehearses songs of orientation,

---

15 Don E. Saliers, *Worship as Theology: Foretaste of Glory Divine* (Nashville: Abingdon Press, 1994), 24.

16 Walter Brueggemann, *The Message of the Psalms: a Theological Commentary* (Minneapolis, MN: Augsburg Press, 1984), 15.

17 Ibid.

18 Examples of orientation psalms would include psalms of creation, such as Psalm 145, 104, 33, and Psalm 8, as well as psalms of the law, wisdom, and retribution.

faith is strengthened; a sense of proper order is affirmed.[19] Psalms of disorientation, which Brueggemann notes are those "most neglected in church use, include songs of deep lament of both personal (Ps 13, 86, 35), and communal nature."[20] Calvin Stapert points out that in Psalm 137 "Israelites sing about being unable to sing."[21] The lament in this psalm confirms not only that the Israelites sang to express their worship, but that singing seemed the only thing adequate to convey their dismay at having lost the full range of singing's own expression. The fact that Jesus used psalms of lament reminds us that he was fully human, and tempted in all points as we are. In his darkest hour, a song from the synagogue falls from His lips. Reggie Kidd states, "In a sense Psalm 22 is the theological center of the book of Psalms."[22] William Willimon reminds us, "Worship helps people not to escape life, but to face it."[23] The psalms demonstrate our singing in the crux of spiritual change. Dietrich Bonhoeffer describes the anguish of the worshiper who crosses the threshold of self-reliance and turns to seek the Divine:

> We can no longer bear it, take it from us and bear it yourself, you alone can handle suffering. That is the goal of all of the lamentation Psalms. They pray concerning the one who took upon himself our diseases and bore our infirmities, Jesus Christ. They proclaim Jesus Christ to be the only help in suffering, for in him God is with us. [24]

Psalms of new orientation include those psalms that reflect the result of God's intervention. The old issue has been overcome.[25] Throughout the psalms that come under this grouping, we find a summons to sing a new

---

19 Theological reflection on psalms of orientation reminds us of the place of humankind in relation to God. In the orientation psalms, we also find evidence and assurance that praise of Yahweh will continue, such as in the affirmation, "from the lips of infants you have ordained praise" (Ps 8:2).

20 See Ps 74, 79, and 137.

21 Calvin R. Stapert, *A New Song in an Old World* (Grand Rapids, MI: Eerdmans Publishing, 2007), 17.

22 Reggie M. Kidd, *With One Voice: Discovering Christ's Song in Our Worship* (Grand Rapids, MI: Baker Books, 2005), 86. Kidd notes, "If the Bible is about utter lostness getting turned around, Psalm 22 tells that story about as compactly and emotively as can be done."

23 William H. Willimon, *Worship as Pastoral Care* (Nashville: Abingdon Press, 1979), 100.

24 Dietrich Bonhoeffer, *Psalms: The Prayer Book of the Bible* (Minneapolis: Augsburg Press, 1970), 48.

25 Brueggemann, *The Message of the Psalms,* 126.

song in response to the refreshment of God's grace. Surely this is the song of the Gospel to be sung by the redeemed.[26] Calvin Stapert argues that this is a much stronger interpretation of the instruction to "sing a new song" (Ps 33) than making that phrase a polemic for changing the repertoire of our worship language. We will address this position more fully later.

According to Brueggemann's description, the life of faith expressed in the Psalms is "focused on the two decisive moves of faith that are always underway, by which we are regularly surprised and which we regularly resist." One move is from orientation to disorientation, and the other is from disorientation to new orientation. In the new place, we are "surprised by a new gift from God, a new coherence made present to us just when we thought all was lost."[27] Delight, amazement, wonder, awe, and gratitude are the natural responses of new orientation, and calls for singing (Jas 5:13). Sadly, it is possible to become complacent to the point that we do not want the stir or revelation that comes with movement. Resistance to spiritual movement would seem to present its own tension in worship, and would affect the dynamics of congregational singing. The song of renewal is often trapped by an underlying attitude of "moralism, or therapeutic deism."[28]

The Psalms demonstrate something of the power of song to pass truth, tradition, and experience on to the next generation. Psalm phrases and expressions continue to show up through pages of the New Testament, repeating and even replenishing the faith expressions of worshipers who have gone before. What is more, the Psalms set a pattern for the worship that casts an eschatological vision.

In review, the central placement of the book of Psalms in the canon reminds us of the centrality of singing faith. Anthropocentric value systems might place certain kinds of emotive expression above others, either out of an interest in serving human art forms, or from interest in using musical expression to speak to base instincts for the purpose of self-attraction. The psalms, on the other hand, reflect the full range of human expression and, as such, indicate the need for the full rule of life to fall submissive to the lordship of Christ, and this condition to be reflected in our singing. The psalms bring together community, give opportunity for the community's expression to God, and speak words to reveal the voice of the Sovereign in

26 Examples of psalms of new orientation include Ps 30, 40, 138, 34, 65, 66, 124, with the later three serving as samples of community thanksgiving.

27 Brueggemann, *The Message of the Psalms,* 20

28 Michael Horton, *Christless Christianity: The Alternative Gospel of the American Church* (Grand Rapids, MI: Baker, 2008), 247.

our singing. The psalms give expression to spiritual condition, including change and surprise. They remind us to sing in light of everlasting hope. The psalms address the identified problem in congregational singing, which is created through an anthropocentric view of worship by assuring that the words we sing have a history of resonating with God as acceptable worship throughout the history of his chosen people. The psalms serve theocentric worship by placing God's word on the lips of worshipers.

MATTHEW 26:30

"When they had sung a hymn, they went out to the Mount of Olives."

This verse, that offers little description of the final moments following the disciples' last meal with Jesus, elicits a myriad of questions. What did the disciples sing? What did Jesus' singing voice sound like? What was the mood and spirit of this singing that brings to a close the time that this band of disciples spent with Jesus in shared communion?

Many scholars seem confident to answer the first question regarding the song. It is no surprise that the song was from the Psalter. Most believe it to have been some, or all of the *Great Hallel* (Ps 115–118), which formed part of the Passover liturgy.[29] The physical sound of Jesus' voice we cannot know, but can only imagine and find a spiritual sense of its timbre as His sheep knowing the voice of the Shepherd (John 10:4). As to the mood and spirit of the singing, we can also only surmise, but D. A. Carson speculates, "Parts of it must have been deeply moving to the disciples when after the Resurrection they remembered that Jesus sang words pledging that he would keep his vows (Ps 116:12–13), ultimately triumph despite rejection (Ps 118), and call all nations to praise Yahweh and his covenant love (Ps 117)."[30]

The singing of the hymn punctuates the *anamnesis* and *prolepsis* of the Supper. Indeed, Craig Blomberg points out the two reasons we continue to worship by taking the meal. "First, we commemorate Jesus' redemptive death. Second, we anticipate his return in company with all the redeemed. These two points remain central to all three Synoptic accounts and should form the heart of any theology of this ordinance."[31] Singing somehow

29 Craig L. Blomberg, "Matthew" in *New American Commentary* (Nashville: Broadman, 1992), 392.

30 D. A. Carson, "Matthew, Mark, Luke" in *The Expositors Bible Commentary,* volume 8 (Grand Rapids, MI: Zondervan, 1984), 539.

31 Blomberg, "Matthew" in *New American Commentary,* 392.

punctuates our worship, and even participates in the *eschaton* by drawing together worship past, worship present, and worship future. Bonhoeffer summarized:

> It is the Christ-hymn, new every morning, that the family fellowship strikes up at the beginning of the day, the hymn that is sung by the whole Church of God on earth and in heaven, and in which we are summoned to join. God has prepared for Himself one great song of praise throughout eternity, and those who enter the community of God join in this song.[32]

Singing is never more emphatic or dramatic than when associated with the Eucharist feast. In a later chapter, we will consider the application and spiritual function of singing during sacred actions in worship.

Reflecting on Matthew 26:30, we may conclude that in our worship singing we hear our Master Shepherd's voice; we remember that he sang, that he will ultimately triumph, and that in the singing, he calls all nations to join the praise. We are reminded that singing punctuates our worship, and most especially, the highest worship of the communion feast, and we are called again to remember our Savior's passion, but also to join with the whole church in singing the Christ hymn that is ever new. All the while, we are moving toward the glorious banquet feast. This single verse demonstrates our Lord's practice of singing within its appropriate and highest value, the worship and glory of God. It is this value that should be revealed when addressing the problem of lesser values that focus on human perception and satisfaction.

I Corinthians 14

The setting of first century Corinth presented a challenging environment for the church's Christian worship, including its singing. Paul's words to the church at Corinth deserve close observation and reflection for application in the practice of congregational singing today, as aspects of that cultural context seem apparent in present day. In Paul's time, Archaean and Hellenistic influences dominated the many worldviews that motivated the people of this human melting pot, where many kinds of spiritualities were practiced. Among the many temples was even a Pantheon dedicated

32 Dietrich Bonhoeffer, *Life Together: The Classic Exploration of Life in Community* (San Francisco: Harper & Row, 1954), 57.

to "all the gods."[33] Singing to one God in this multi-god pluralistic context seems a challenge not unlike present-day reality.

The Corinthian church was primarily comprised of Gentile believers, some of whom apparently engaged in the same practices that could be observed in the rest of the Corinthian culture. James Blevins observes, however, that "the most pressing problem was that of division in their ranks—some belonged to Paul, others to Apollos, Cephas, or Christ." The many voices of spirituality outside the church seem to have made their way into the church along with the converts. Rather than recognizing their blindness to the duplicity of multiple theologies juxtaposed with spiritual pride, Corinthians may have seen themselves as "a Christ party set above others in the Church."[34]

Gerald Borchert concludes, "The Corinthians' self interest in the matters of worship and 'spirituality' prevented them from achieving maturity and truncated their church life."[35] It is no surprise that among the many problems and issues of the Corinthian church, Paul lays his foremost address to the issue of unity. His instruction regarding worship in chapter fourteen is reflective of the priority of love that had been clearly established in chapter thirteen. Paul begins the fourteenth chapter with the imperative, "Pursue love" (v.1). This spirit undergirds singing. Worship is always doxological, but David Nelson points to this passage to remind us, "It is not enough to build up oneself in worship. We must always ask whether our doxological actions encourage the edification of the whole church" (vv. 4, 13–17, 26).[36]

Paul asks us to sing with head and heart in worship (v.15). Robert Webber indicates the "head and heart" tension in worship is "the tension between *spirituality* and *theology*."[37] David Garland states, "When one speaks rationally with the mind, it does not necessarily mean that the spirit lies fallow or that the Spirit does not inspire."[38] He notes that 1 Corinthians1:10, and Romans 12:2, call worshipers to be of "one *mind*"

33 James L. Blevins, "Introduction to 1 Corinthians" in *Review & Expositor* 80 (1983), 317.

34 Ibid., 320–321.

35 Gerald Borchert, *New Testament Reflections on Worship: Divine Glory and Human Response* (Morristown, TN: Chalice Press, 2007), 103.

36 David P. Nelson, "Voicing God's Praise" in *Authentic Worship*, ed. Herbert W. Bateman IV (Grand Rapids, MI: Kregel Academic & Professional, 2002), 151.

37 Robert E. Webber, *Worship Old & New* (Grand Rapids, MI: Zondervan, 1994), 114–115.

38 David E. Garland, "I Corinthians" in *Baker Exegetical Commentary on the New Testament* (Grand Rapids, MI: Baker Academic, 2003), 640.

and for the *mind* to be transformed. On the other hand, if the mind is active without the spirit, then worship remains "theoretical." Garland believes the ultimate point for our worship, and in this case, singing as an act of worship, is "… spiritual ecstasy [that] will be complemented by rational interpretation that communicates to others and produces fruit."[39]

Paul addresses a need for the understandability of worship language for the benefit of the non-believer (vv. 23–25). His concern gives evidence that worship, and therefore singing in worship, can certainly serve as a vehicle for Gospel witness. The singing indicated in this passage presents an interesting complexity to the issue of singing as worship, since unbelievers cannot worship in the sense that believers do, but in the case of congregational singing, unbelievers would be hearing the Gospel through the singing of the church and, in a sense, potentially even in their own voice. It is possible for the church to sing purposefully its witness in and through its worship.

Paul's address to the church in 1 Corinthians 14 is an address regarding worship practice, order, and spirit in a cultural environment similar to present day. It seems logical to make application of his instructive concerns to the congregational singing practice in worship today. Characteristics of our worship singing, therefore, include avoiding spiritual pride, pursuing love, edifying the church, singing with our mind and heart, and all of this is done in an understandable manner that we might bear witness to the Gospel of Christ through our worship and singing. The characteristics indicated in 1 Corinthians 14 address directly problematic singing that finds pride in its own performance, style, or presumed ability to "draw" unbelievers by its own intrinsic worth. Study of this passage should assist worship leadership in centering worship singing on Christ rather than on anthropocentric values.

Ephesians 5:19–20 and Colossians 3:15–17

Paul's letters to the churches at Ephesus and Colosse indicate they are already engaged in singing together in worship. In the Ephesians passage, the instruction regarding songs and singing follows the directive to "be filled with the Spirit" (vs. 18). F. F. Bruce notes a cause-and-effect relationship: "If the Spirit is the source of their fullness, then their mouths will be filled with words which build up the lives of others and bring glory to the living and true God." Likewise, in the Colossians passage, Bruce recognizes, "The meetings of those early Christians must have been musical

39 Ibid.

occasions, as they not only sang and made melody to the Lord, in their hearts as well as with their tongues, but addressed one another for mutual help and blessing in compositions already known to the community or in songs improvised under immediate inspiration."[40]

Colossians 3:16's reference to allowing the Word of Christ to "dwell in you" gives rise to a question that has potential for profound effect on the mindset of congregational singing as worship, especially transposed in today's society's strong emphasis on a personal spirituality. The issue is whether the "in you" refers to individual believers or to the community of believers. Herbert Bateman contends, "Perhaps it would be unwise to rule either alternative out completely, although the collective sense may be uppermost in view of the context."[41] Recognition of holy presence in worship can serve as a control over misplaced consumption with privatized worship moments and non-attention to the worshiping community with which we have gathered.

Don Hustad believes the three genres of music mentioned in Paul's letters to the Ephesians and Colossians were different "in origin, in subject matter, and possibly even in performance practice."[42] Whether or not the genres mentioned in these verses are intended to cover the sum of worship music repertoire, it would seem clear that their inclusion indicates that worship singing encompassed many means of conveying praise to God and edification of his church.

From these passages, we glean that worship singing is connected to the spiritual condition of being filled with the Spirit, and that through Spirit-led singing, God is glorified and the church is built up. We see that singing is best done when conditioned by the Word living in and among us. We also conclude from this passage that many means of singing express worship and edification, including remembered songs, theological praise songs, and songs of jubilation, each sung according to its designation. Careful attention to singing in the spirit of Paul's instruction in these two letters would appear to confront problematic attitudes that would pit the singing of one genre against another.

---

40 F. F. Bruce, "The Epistles to the Colossians, Philemon and the Ephesians" in *The New International Commentary on the New Testament* (Grand Rapids, MI: Eerdmans Publishing, 1984), 380–381.

41 Herbert Bateman, *Authentic Worship: Hearing Scripture's Voice, Applying the Truth* (Grand Rapids, MI: Kregel Academic & Professional, 2002), 157.

42 Don Hustad, *Jubilate II: Church Music in Worship and Renewal* (Carol Stream, IL: Hope Publishing, 1993), 146–147.

Hebrews 10:19–25

The access that the believer has to the throne is foundational for singing in faith as worship. The writer of Hebrews exhorts and invites not only to "draw near," but to do so with boldness. Prior to verse nineteen, the writer has provided his argument that the object of faith is the fully sufficient sacrifice of Christ through his blood. It is His (Christ's) work that has provided the means by which we "approach the throne with boldness" (vs. 19). Our singing is empowered by his faith and his work. "We cannot blunder into the presence of the Almighty on our own terms."[43] The worshiper approaches through the One High Priest, Jesus Christ. He welcomes and gathers us into the "house of God" (vs. 21), which includes all worshipers of God for all time. Reverting back to David Peterson's definition of worship and our starting point in our theological reflection, this One High Priest, this holy sacrifice, is the avenue of our worship on the "terms he (God) proposes and the means he provides."[44] "By the blood of Christ, we have boldness to enter into the holiest place, a place that struck terror into the hearts of Old Testament believers."[45] Through Christ in boldness we sing our worship! This is our freedom!

Congregational singing assumes assembly. Group singing only occurs after the grouping has taken place. The writer of Hebrews exhorts believers to assemble together. Assembly [*episunagoogeen*] is only found here and 2 Thessalonians 2:1 (the gathering together of the elect to Christ at His coming, Matt 24:31). Charles Trentham notes that the preacher of Hebrews demonstrates a recurring emphasis on the *eschaton*.[46] The unity of faith is strengthened as "continual assemblings beget and foster love, and give opportunities for 'provoking to good works,' by 'exhorting one another'" (Heb 3:13). Ignatius exhorts, "When ye frequently and in numbers meet together, the powers of Satan are overthrown, and his mischief is neutralized by your like-mindedness in the faith."[47] In our like-mindedness, we spur one another on to good works.

---

43 Charles A. Trentham, *Broadman Bible Commentary: Hebrews* (Nashville: Broadman Publishing, 1972), 74.

44 Peterson, *Engaging with God,* 20.

45 John Frame, *Contemporary Worship Music: A Biblical Defense* (Phillipsburg, NJ: P&R Publishing, 1997), 15.

46 Charles A. Trentham, *Broadman Bible Commentary, Hebrews* (Nashville, TN: Broadman Press, 1972), 74–75.

47 Robert Jamieson, Andrew Fausset, and David Brown, *A Commentary: Critical, Experimental, and Practical on the Old and New Testaments* (Grand Rapids, MI: Eerdmans, 1993) reproduced in *PC Study Bible 5* [CD-ROM] (Seattle, WA: Biblesoft, 2006).

The passage exhorts us to sing in faith, and that faith clearly not centered in ourselves, but in the provision of Christ. Our singing is to be confident because of Christ, even bold as we come to God in worship. Our singing joins the ongoing song of the "house of God," and assumes our assembly, but advocates continuous assembling in which we will encourage one another toward good works until Christ returns. Surely, this passage speaks to congregational singing leaders to be aware of the gathered body in the singing of our worship. For singing to fulfill the spirit of exhorting one another to "good works," we must surely pay attention to who the "one another" are that are present, and to whether or not they are engaged in the singing.

Revelation 5:9–13 and 15:1–3

John's vision into the heavenly realm includes music and singing of praise in the presence of the One who was present at the first singing when morning stars and angels sang together (Job 38:7). Creatures and elders join the many angels (Rev 5: 11) in singing the song of praise of the Worthy Lamb who is fully deserving of worship. Morris Ashcraft comments that the acts of worship revealed here "show the Christian belief that Christ is deserving the same kind of worship given to God."[48] Amid harps and golden bowls of incense (Rev. 5:8) comes the "new song" in which Christ is appropriately lifted up. The worship has come full circle in this vision where we find that the song being sung into eternity continues the song of deliverance. In heaven, the picture John paints for us includes white robes and sounds of victory. "They stand by the heavenly Red Sea and sing the song of Moses; they have been delivered."[49] They sing the "song of the Lamb," who delivers us not only to safety, but to ultimate victory.

Writing a theology of the church, Mark Dever states, "Ultimately, the praises of the Christian assembly on earth foreshadow the praise that will be offered in heaven."[50] Christian worship centers in, is made possible by, and is only available through the work of the slain, resurrected, and enthroned Christ. The song that is sung in verse thirteen is the new song "to him who sits upon the throne and to the Lamb," where "both God and Christ are conjoined in the doxology."[51]

48 Morris Ashcraft, "Revelation" in *The Broadman Bible Commentary* (Nashville: Broadman Press, 1972), 282.

49 Ibid., 322.

50 Mark E. Dever, "The Church" in *A Theology for the Church* (Nashville, TN: B&H Academic, 2007), 810.

51 F. F. Bruce, *The Epistles to the Colossians, to Philemon, and to the Ephesians,* 381.

From these visions in Revelation, we are reminded of the continuing nature of our singing as response to the nature and presence of God. We are presented with the theme of His deliverance, and are reminded of the victorious tone that must be sounded as an ever-recurring dynamic of our singing in theocentric worship.[52] We are once again confronted with the reality of our position in worship, bowing down to the one worthy to receive honor, and power, and blessing, and to whom one day "every knee shall bow and every tongue confess that Jesus Christ is Lord." The value of our singing for now and to eternity is found in the worship of the Worthy Lamb.

The passages of Scripture mentioned above provide an overview of biblical reference to singing. There are many more that reflect everything from the grand pageantry of the temple dedication in 2 Chronicles 7, to the intimate playing and singing of David that cast a healing effect on King Saul in 1 Samuel, to the witness of two prisoners singing hymns in the darkness of prison in Acts 16. Scripture reveals our identity as a "chosen people, a royal priesthood, a holy nation, a people belonging to God, that you may declare the praises of him who called you out of darkness into his wonderful light" (1 Pet 2:9). As we sing our praises, we affirm and continue to reform our identity. Our song and our singing must always be measured by the written Word.

A History of Struggle – To Sing or Not to Sing

From the earliest days of the Ancient Church, music, including singing, has proven to be a formidable issue for church leadership. Questions of cultural context and conflicts over instrumentation issues have been serious considerations. Even after Constantinople formalized the relationship of church with the state and sought to normalize Christianity with culture, questions continued as to whether music's influence and governance was from without or within the church. Singing, or any form of music, has been included in worship, then ousted from worship, then included again over the course of church history. Questions of its appropriateness and efficacy are anything but new.

52 Canticles, referring to those texts in the Bible that were sung, especially those other than the Psalms, included songs we now see in the Old and New Testament. The *Benedictus* (Luke 1:68–79), *Magnificat* (Luke 1:46–55), *Gloria in Excelsis* (Luke 2:14), *Nunc Dimittis* (Luke 2:29–32) may be added to the *Song of Moses* and *Worthy Lamb* texts that have already been mentioned. Many other *hymns* can be found throughout Scripture. Discussions of the canticles and Christological hymns can be found in Paul Westermeyer's *Te Deum: The Church and Music* (Minneapolis: Fortress Press, 1998), and Don P. Hustad's *Jubilate II: Church Music in the Evangelical Tradition* (Carol Stream, IL: Hope Publishing, 1998).

Augustine struggled to know the divine will concerning music when he confessed that the "pleasures of the ear had a more tenacious hold on me, and had subjugated me." The church father also realized, however, the value of sung words as he noted, "When they are sung with a clear voice and entirely appropriate modulation, then again I recognize the great utility of music in worship."[53] Through the second and third centuries, it is most likely that the church had no choirs, but had only the congregation's singing led by a cantor. The cantor's identity was so obscure that it is suggested that it was "anonymous and only gradually comes into view in the fourth century."[54] Ambrose of Milan sought music's re-introduction into the worship of the church after its exclusion by previous leaders.[55] He has been credited with introducing antiphonal chant to the Latin Church and is sometimes called the "father of church song."[56] Clement of Alexandria opposed chromatic modes, but allowed the development of choirs and more elaborate *troparia* (hymnlike chants) as well as canons.

These developments meant someone had to give consideration to musical concerns. That consideration would seem to introduce three particular tensions to the worship. First, the very focus of such attention to crafting music for worship, at whatever level; second, the influence of the one tending to such matters; and third, the music's own influence as art expression. Legend has it that an Egyptian abbot named Pambo sent a disciple to Alexandria where he observed the liturgy. The disciple was moved by what he experienced to a point of dissatisfaction with the lack of use of music in his own worship. Following his return, Pambo is said to have called for silence in the church seeing as how this distraction called affection away from the Holy Spirit. Paul Westermeyer points out that details on the life and writing of Pambo are elusive. They are important, nonetheless, in that the antidote represents a way of dealing with music and singing that has been adopted repeatedly as a solution to issues of music's influence, whether thought of as idolatrous, distracting, or sensuous sinfulness.[57]

---

53 St. Augustine, *Confessions X,* xxxiii, 49–50; 207–208.

54 Edward Foley, "The Cantor in Historical Perspective," *Worship 56:3* (May 1982), 194–213.

55 Donald Jay Grout, *A History of Western Music,* third edition (New York: Norton & Company, 1980), 17–18, 26–27. Grout credits Bishop Ambrose of Milan with introducing antiphonal psalmody to the West, as well as contributing songs later known as Ambrosian chant.

56 Paul Westermeyer, *Te Deum: The Church and Music* (Minneapolis: Fortress Press, 1998), 82–83.

57 Ibid., 84–89.

At the risk of over-simplification, three lines of thought seem to become prevalent among church leaders in the early centuries regarding the practice of music in the church's worship: the complete exclusion of music in worship (Pambo), full acceptance of music (Ambrose), and an inclusion of music with conditional restraint (Augustine).

In the Reformation, we can find philosophies similar to the three just mentioned regarding music's inclusion in worship. Like Ambrose, Martin Luther embraced music, and even elevated it second only to the Word of God. He believed singing offered opportunity to participate in a reflection of the beauty of God's great creation. Like Pambo, Ulrich Zwingli denied congregational singing in worship. He led in radical response to some of the excesses of the middle ages, even to the point of burning choir books, smashing statues, and whitewashing art-covered church buildings. Other reformers parted fellowship over the "right" music for worship. John Calvin first banned music from worship, but later recanted and the Geneva reformer allowed metrical psalms sung in unison by the congregation.[58] Calvin's provisional acceptance is not unlike Augustine's caution in order that attention and affection would remain seeded in God's Word through the use of music in worship.

Throughout history and to the present day, the church musician has been faced with the question of the extent to which ministry practice decisions would be based on aestheticism verses pragmatism.[59] The basis of such decisions has great effect on the direction of congregational singing, accordingly. Is our singing to reflect *imago dei* by giving our best in singing beautifully? Are we to *use* music to achieve a kind of spiritual result? Is our music to somehow balance these directions? Continual attention to the controlling point of worship's adornments appears to be an ever-present dynamic with which music leaders must contend.

As a Baptist, I have found enrichment through the study of faith traditions different than my own. Those traditions that rely on prescribed liturgy provide a means by which worship history can be studied through those prescribed liturgies, observing their development over years. Congregational music in these environments rightly tends to support the

---

58 Don Hustad, *Jubilate II,* 535.

59 Calvin M. Johansson, *Music & Ministry: A Biblical Counterpoint,* (Peabody MA: Hendrickson Publishers, 1984), 8. Johansson posits that "God cannot be contained by propositional statements," but recognizes that paradoxes in our limited understandings, even seeming contradictions can show fuller truth in relationship to each other in "a beautiful contrapuntal design which is the philosophical basis of a pastoral music ministry."

ethos prescribed. On the other hand, Pentecostal and charismatic traditions that rely upon immediate revelation tend to produce music of high emotive consequence and pursue experience. The struggle of aestheticism verses pragmatism is sometimes more easily understood through reviewing its tensions within churches other than your own. A review of Baptist worship reveals similar tensions regarding the proper material, demeanor, and motivation for music and singing in church worship.

Baptists and Congregational Singing

The earliest record of Baptist worship in 1609 gives no indication of music whatsoever, congregational singing or otherwise.[60] Baptist history is marked with divisions and schisms, but in large part, two streams of theological dispositions can be noted that eventually flow into what became the Southern Baptist Convention. These streams are important to the discussion of worship singing, as distinct worship ethos developed around these streams. General Baptists, more Arminian in theological emphasis, worshiped in a way so as not to quench the Spirit, which, in that emphasis, meant avoiding "prescribed worship." Baptist scholar and statesman, David Dockery notes that these Baptists, led by John Smyth and Thomas Helwys, "were dedicated to what might be called 'spiritual worship,' which was accompanied by a commitment to flexibility and change."[61] No books, including songbooks, would have been allowed in this worship, as anything compiled might be viewed as limiting the freedom of the Spirit. They would have viewed the *Common Book of Prayer,* for instance, as incompatible to spirited worship.

Particular Baptists, on the other hand, would have been given to a more formal environment and controlled demeanor to go along with their Calvinist theology and its emphasis on order. A hymnal for congregational singing, which would organize and bring unity of form in worship expression, was advocated by Particular Baptist pastor Benjamin Keach in 1691.[62] Dockery notes a merging of these streams into a spirited formality that he calls a "British tradition" for Baptists, which seems to be the ethos of Baptist worship in colonial America. He correctly notes the "tension

60 H. Leon McBeth, *The Baptist Heritage: Four Centuries of Baptist Witness* (Nashville, TN: Broadman Press, 1987), 91.

61 David S. Dockery, *Southern Baptist Consensus and Renewal: A Biblical, Historical, and Theological Proposal* (Nashville: B&H Academic, 2008), 103.

62 Don Hustad, *Jubilate II,* 203. Keach was reportedly the first to introduce hymns in addition to psalms to an English congregation.

between form and freedom." This tension is an ever-present dynamic of any music in worship, including congregational singing.

The singing in the frontier revival movement in America was often spontaneous and was "designed to bring about an emotional response."[63] A group of Baptist churches in North Carolina, given to this highly emotional ethos in worship, formed the Sandy Creek Baptist Association, named for its location. The emotional intention of the Sandy Creek tradition is a dynamic of congregational singing that continues, consciously and unconsciously, in the discussions and tensions of Baptist worship.

A more Calvinist, more stately, and formal environment became known as the Charleston tradition of Baptist worship. It was deemed such in reference to one of the first churches of its ilk, First Baptist Church, Charleston, South Carolina, along with the association of churches that were of similar piety. The singing in churches of the Charleston tradition tended toward a more prepared and musically-informed practice.

Though sung with different levels of flare and musicality, some texts and hymnody were shared by churches of these two streams. Watts and the Wesleys had profound influence on all Baptist worship singing both before and following great spiritual movements in the United Kingdom and in America. Convergence of streams of Baptist life have made for continued tensions related to worship expressions as theological emphases have tended to be supported, not only by a type of hymnody, but by different pieties in the worship singing itself. Over the course of time, it would appear that the piety in the singing, or a preference for a particular ethos connected to a kind of singing, may have rendered the theological positions with which they were first associated of secondary importance in practice. In most cases, aspects of the recent so-called worship wars are largely rooted in music's value system whether from the world of art, academia, or commercialism,[64] rather than from theological reflection. Content, form, and ways of singing that might be better understood as anthropocentric or theocentric may not be consistent with the theological conservatism of a church or pastor, or with their inclination to a Calvinist verses Arminian position.

In review, Baptist singing, like Baptist life, seems to have always been practiced in the midst of tensions over a variety of theological and practical

63 Ibid., 106.

64 Harold M. Best, *Music Through the Eyes of Faith* (New York: Harper Publishers, 1993), 41–51. Also see Terry W. York, *American Worship Wars* (Peabody, MA: Hendrickson Publishers, 2003) and Thomas G. Long, *Beyond the Worship Wars: Building Vital and Faithful Worship* (Bethesda, MD: Alban Institute, 2000), 53–64.

issues. The tension of formality verses informality, with respective ethos and assumed prejudices, has been part of Baptist worship history, though most of that history is not recorded as such. Tensions that paralleled cultural periods have been reflected in Baptist worship singing. The so-called enlightenment period and resultant modernist thinking influenced congregational singing that tended to seek either intellectual superiority or experiential justification. The postmodern context, which thus far has resulted in multi-faceted singing environments, has shown signs of syncretism and individualism.[65] Ongoing influences of culture in general, and foundational value systems on which singing ethos might be based in particular, have influenced and continue to influence the dynamics of singing in Baptist worship.

It seems highly important that those leading congregational singing as worship would comprehend the theological streams and historical foundation of pieties within which congregational singing takes place in worship. Such comprehension would serve a deepened understanding of the dynamics of such singing, which we have sought to show addresses the problem of conflicting value systems and misappropriated controlling points for leading congregational singing in worship. Embedded philosophies and theologies among members of a congregation, as well as those among the leadership, may be consistent with practice, and/or may conflict with practice when underpinned by different value systems.

Theological Implications for Congregational Singing

The biblical examples of group singing show us that God's presence and actions evoke response. In this singing, there is a recurring theme of God's deliverance, which inspires the human spirit either to offer praise or to cry out for that deliverance. Biblical instruction regarding worship and singing emphasizes an attitude of love. It indicates order, teaching, encouragement, and concern for one another above self. The narrative calls for a sensitivity to non-believers who might be present in public worship, and an emphasis on faithful gathering for worship which includes singing. The biblical record shows the eternal nature of praise in the apocalyptic

65 Robert E. Webber, *Ancient-Future Faith: Rethinking Evangelicalism for a Postmodern World* (Grand Rapids, MI: Baker Books, 1999), 99. Webber's discussion presents a clear picture of how modern and postmodern thought systems influence style, which then becomes a priority consideration of worship above a biblical theology of worship.

vision that again reveals that in the presence of God there is singing, even singing for eternity.

My brief summary of the church's historic struggle over music actually portrays something of the nature of the human condition under the fall. The congregation's singing is perhaps especially vulnerable to struggle. Aspects of singing that render it effective in its work in worship and spiritual expression also render congregational singing potent for misunderstanding, manipulation, and in the worse case, outright deceit.

It is important to advance the discussion of the effect of singing with consideration of the basic components of our singing, words and music, which we will attempt to do in chapters four and five. Congregational singing occurs as a result of a fundamental reality of the church, its gathering. I would therefore note that for worship through congregational singing to be complete, it must include a comprehension of ecclesiology. The biblical imperative of assembly is to be shaped by loving concern for those gathered and finds aspects of its efficacy in forming the community that joins in the singing. This may even provide one means of recognizing worship renewal. "We will take steps away from our secularly influenced and individualistic emphases to concentrate on the whole body, so that all things will be done for mutual edification (see 1 Cor 14:26)."[66]

For leadership of congregational singing to be theologically sound, it seems necessary that those doing the leading should continue to deepen their understanding of congregational singing dynamics. Worship renewal can only be served if such a deepening is approached in light of biblical revelation and historical perspective in a spirit of servanthood to Christ and His church. Theologically sound congregational singing, inspired and quickened by the Holy Spirit in theocentric worship, is surely the desire of those who would serve as the "royal priesthood" (1 Pet 2:9).

---

66 David Dockery, *Southern Baptist Consensus and Renewal*, 128.

Chapter 3

UNISON AND HARMONY – NOT ALL WORSHIP GATHERINGS ARE ALIKE

The worship music leader admonished us worshipers to mentally draw an imaginary circle around ourselves and then to close our eyes, effectively leaving each of us in our own worship silo. As the electronic keyboard sustained a chord on a soft string pad sound, the leader strummed his guitar somewhat randomly and spoke with breathy tones into the microphone, instructing us to allow only images of Jesus and ourselves to fill our mind. I was a visitor in the service, there to make connection with this musician who had only recently moved to our area. The manipulative technique was off-putting for me. Much more importantly, it seemed to beg those who had presumably come to worship in community to drop that notion as if to pretend we had all stayed home but found a quiet corner in which to worship. Following the service, I took the worship leader to lunch and asked about the technique, seeking to create a climate for self-evaluation, and to gently encourage honest assessment. His response to my question was of equal concern. He told me, "The truth is that these people don't know how to worship. For many of them, this is probably the only time they really focus on Jesus, and it is my responsibility to lead them to the throne. For some of them, this is the only way they will know how to talk with Jesus, and the only time they will be alone with Him."

I did not know exactly how to respond to the exchange I had with this worship leader. I did not want my contrary reflection to hinder any opportunity for meaningful fellowship with this brother whose well-meaning I felt was misguided. I affirmed his sense of responsibility to teach people concepts of worship, but I really wanted to help him think differently about the worship gathering. When I asked him about the level of community within this very large congregation, he seemed to be at complete loss as to my meaning. I immediately determined we would both be better served if I worked at developing our relationship before any theological conceptualizing. I saved the pontification for a much later time.

Trinitarian worship by its nature is an engagement of community. We have already noted that Christian worship is an engagement with God, a communion or communication taking place between a triune God and His creation, human beings. On God's side of this equation, there is a triune being, "God in three persons, blessed Trinity." There have been numerous attempts at allegorizing the Trinity in efforts to assist our understanding of this deepest of mysteries. The three-in-one nature of God presents a fascinating dynamic of worship. Precisely because of His threefold nature, it is possible to recognize Him as a community. The Holy Spirit is in us as we worship. Christ has come into our lives, and lives in our hearts, and has stated that where two or three are gathered in His Name, He is present among us.

Sadly, much of present day worship practice in churches, including churches of my own denomination, could be identified as what James Torrance calls "functionally Unitarian."[1] In this view, worship is something that we humans do. God has blessed us, and as response, we want to thank Him and respond with our religious duty, worship. In effect, we seek to give God our attention, hoping He will give us His. We pray for our lives to be better, intercede for one another and those outside our fellowship, and listen to a sermon that we trust is a word from the Lord. Torrance says we sit in the pew watching the minister "do his thing," exhorting us to "do our thing," and then we leave feeling we have done our duty for another week. This "God and me" worship, such as that encouraged in the silo mentality offered in the opening example, seems to hold little reliance on, much less

1 James B. Torrance, *Worship, Community and the Triune God of Grace,* (Downers Grove, IL: InterVarsity Press, 1996), 20.

engagement in, what is taking place in the Godhead. In a Unitarian view of worship, there is no doctrine of the Holy Spirit drawing us into the communion between Son and Father. In Unitarian worship, we are left to serve as our own mediator and priest, rather than placing our reliance upon the High Priest, Jesus Christ, the Supreme Worship Leader, whose sacrifice is the only means by which we can approach the Holy of Holies.

If worship is indeed a "twenty-four-seven" engagement, it seems inevitable that it will occur in different groupings of persons. James Torrance notes, "When we, who know we are God's creatures, worship God together, we gather up the worship of all creation." The focus on community captures the focus of the biblical message, stands at the heart of the theological heritage of the church, and "it speaks to the aspirations and the sensed needs of people in our world today." Stanley Grenz notes, "As we realize we are created for community, we are in a position to connect Christian belief with Christian living." [2]

Engaging in Trinitarian worship means that even so-called private worship, or worship in solitude, involves a worshiping community that includes at a minimum Father, Son, Spirit, and the believer. While privatized worship has been the pentacle of the focus for many modern churches—where *personal* relationship with Christ trumps all spiritual grouping considerations—all worship gatherings deserve careful attention as to their contribution to the larger picture of bringing glory to God through Christ in the cultic activity we know as Christian worship. There are obvious larger physical gatherings to consider beyond this smallest worship grouping, of course. I want you to consider four such groupings; solitude, family or small group, congregational or church worship, and festival worship. We will consider each separately and then ponder how each makes a contribution to the holistic life of worship for the larger body of Christ, the universal church, and for each individual believer.

Determining what songs to sing, and how to sing them in various groupings, is a challenge. Pulling or pushing away from community, such as that indicated in the opening illustration, is antithetical to what it means to engage in Trinitarian worship. The terminology needed to describe these groupings will take its meaning from the number of human persons that are physically present in each setting.

---

2 Stanley Grenz, *Created for Community: Connecting Christian Belief with Christian Living* (Grand Rapids, MI: Baker Books, 1998), 23.

Worship in Solitude – private worship

Private worship, or worship in solitude, is the first grouping I would like to discuss. For some people, worship in isolation is the height of what it means to worship God. The solitude of worship which seems exclusive in that only the single worshiper gathers with the Triune God may find many means of expression, and a variety of places for the gathering itself. Worship of this sort may be as intentional as a daily quiet time where we purposefully slip to a designated place secluded from the busyness of our world. Worship of this sort, however, may just as well present itself in a sort of opportunistic fashion, such as what happens often to me when I am driving away from the office headed on a business trip and realize that the drive itself will last a number of hours. In the course of the drive, I may engage in singing praise with little restriction, or I may play a CD as loudly as serves moments of inspiration and reflection. God may meet me on a crisp fall morning jog or in the backyard when I am celebrating a freshly mown lawn as the fruit of an afternoon's labor.

Much has been written about the need for regular pulling away from the busyness of life to find solace, to simply "be still and know" that He is God. Professor and theologian, Syd Hielema, reminds us, "In solitude and silence we are able to listen for the presence of God, listen to the sounds of our own spirits, step outside of the symphony (or cacophony) of our routines, and discern more clearly the shape of their melodies, harmonies, and textures."[3] Many religious leaders of every decade have been known to spend much time stolen away in a quiet place for worship, prayer, and silent meditation.

Worship singing for private or personal worship is not limited to those like me who are musicians by training. Most of us have occasioned the earbud-laidened airport dweller, who has forgotten the boundary of his life space and begun to sing to match the level of the rock band that is screaming in his ears. A deficit of pitch-matching ability does not usually deter him from enjoying his chosen music out loud if he is lost in the music. Such activity is usually predicated on a desire to be isolated into a controlled environment that allows escape from a given atmosphere (like the airport terminal), to be able to flood the ears, mind, and subsequent emotions with a mood of choice. Many Christians seem to have need of constant noise in searching for inspiration to move them toward a sense of nearness to God. While playing the music of Christian artists may drown

3 Syd Hielema "The Festival-Envy Syndrome" in *Reformed Worship,* March, 2004, 4.

out some of the world's distractions, if we are not careful, it may cover the "still small voice" of God Himself. Worship communion in solitude would seem to be well served at times by the discipline of silence.

Henri Nouwen reflects upon the teachings of the desert fathers, reminding us that "silence guards the fire within."[4] While my intention in this work is to consider the application of worship singing, an effective prelude for any verbal expression through worship in solitude is a time of silence. Such silence need not be presumed in too literal of a sense. Abba Poem states, "A man may seem to be silent, but if his heart is condemning others he is babbling ceaselessly. But there may be another who talks from morning till night and yet he is truly silent."[5]

Singing during a time of private worship provides an opportunity for our most intimate expressions. Such intimacy and passionate expression need not be confined to the intimacy expressed in the lyric itself. Certainly, singing "I Love You, Lord" or "How Great Thou Art" can be moments of deeply personal praise expressions. Songs of great theological truth, however, may also find new resonance as we express them paired with no other audible voices, but rather recognize that we are known to the Lord, who has "searched and known me" (Ps. 139). Our hymning of the "Immortal, Invisible, God, Only Wise" may strengthen our understanding of our own place among the throng of those who "Worship the King," who is "pavilioned in splendor and girded with praise."

When I was serving in local church music ministry and was building a youth choir program, I found it strategically beneficial to develop a select ensemble comprised of members from the youth choir. My philosophy was to choose singers for this group through an audition process who had superior musical skills and whose voice timbres matched well enough to produce a homogenous ensemble. While the ensemble provided talented musicians with additional opportunities for music making and provided an additional ensemble that could be selected to sing for service music, this was not usually the highest contribution of this select group. Rather, I found that as I worked to develop a unique sound among these select voices and advanced their ability to balance and blend with one another, they began to listen for one another in the larger ensemble of the youth choir, and thus advanced the sound of that group. They often informed

---

4 Henri Nouwen, *The Way of the Heart: Connecting with God through Prayer, Wisdom, and Silence* (New York: Ballantine Books, 1981), 45.

5 Benedicta Ward, trans., *The Sayings of the Desert Fathers* (London & Oxford: Mowbrays, 1975), 143.

me that they listened intently for one another and most weeks could hear the twelve to fifteen voices of the ensemble among the fifty or sixty of the larger choir. This same principal can apply in a spiritual sense as we better know our own voice expressed in private worship, and as we know what it is to sing with a smaller family group and seek to blend with those voices within the larger choir of the congregation or in a festival setting.

Hearing our own voice express unbridled praise when singing as an expression of our worship when no other person is physically present may very well help to free us to express our worship as part of the larger body of the congregation or other worship grouping when we gather with others. Better yet, as we sense that Jesus sings His worship with us, we may become better worshiping sheep who "know His voice" (John 10:27).

The song sung in private worship may be a song given anew in the moment. As an occasional songwriter, I would note that spontaneous singing in a private worship setting may open the heart to a new song that grows out of the experience of the moment itself. Better yet, the words of the Word of God may find a spontaneous melody and rhythm in these moments of meditation and praise.

Family worship

Most churches are made up of small groups inside the larger congregation. In addition to the nuclear families, congregations encourage gatherings of senior adults, newlywed couples, young parents, and singles. Many who attend church find important and meaningful relationship through such groupings. High school students attend specially-planned fellowships following Friday night football games, attend concerts and camps for youth, and participate in retreats that are designed specifically to address developmental teen issues. Leaders expose teenagers to the music of Christian artists by organizing trips to concerts or promoting recordings of their favorite artists. Adult workers prepare times of worship for children and youth groups. Senior adults enjoy covered dish fellowships and share life experiences through organized leisure travel. Sunday school classes of all ages participate in periodic fellowship gatherings.

Church choirs and other service ministry groups within the congregation provide environments that develop relationship among members who experience regular gatherings and find occasions to share life. I have attended many funerals where eulogies were delivered by a fellow choir member, deacon, or a fellow member of the disaster relief team who served alongside of the one being remembered. Serving Christ, the church, and community tends to build a depth in relationships.

Gatherings of affinity groups such as those mentioned above provide unique opportunities for worship and worship singing. When I was a kid, adult Sunday school classes organized into departments and spent the first fifteen minutes of the Bible Study hour on Sunday morning singing, sharing and praying for needs, and organizing to contact those absent. Small group gatherings of this sort provided opportunity for young piano players and music leaders to obtain experience leading groups to sing worship. Many who serve on church staffs today bear testimony to getting their start by playing, leading, and singing for these small group gatherings.

Today, youth praise bands emulate the bands they hear on Christian radio or that they experience while attending artist concerts in area churches or concert halls. Youth leaders would do well to be certain that music used for worship singing does not simply feature the band's performance, but rather gives rise to participation through worship singing and edifies the worshipers present. Many youth leaders encourage teens to listen to particular artists in their own leisure listening. I have known youth ministers who frequently publish song lists to tell their students what was playing on their own iPods. Certainly, such action can prepare worshipers for gathered worship that includes those same teens in family worship.

Syd Hielema notes that the extended family worship environment is distinguished by its ability to deepen interpersonal relationships. One reason for this distinction is the affinity of such groupings, which are often of similar life posture by design. Parenting groups, the afore-mentioned age groupings, or ministry task groups are all environments where like interests and needs provide a basis for transparency and vulnerability that is not available to larger gatherings. A natural intimacy may develop quickly in settings where parents are mutually concerned for their children and may experience common needs of wisdom in their roles of life responsibility. Such affinity seems to foster an atmosphere conducive to intimate expression.

I have personally known church choir rehearsals to be ripe environments for extended family worship. There is something about connecting our musical sensitivity with the music-making process applied to spiritually rich texts, while seeking to sense such art's mood together as a choir, that strips away layers of prideful facades behind which we often live our daily lives. Worship expression seems inevitable from a group that seeks to be purposeful in developing its own sensitivity to spiritual activity as part of its skill development process. I have had the privilege of being present when a choir member recognized their own lost condition in a rehearsal setting. I have been involved in numerous choir retreats when worship opened the gates of heaven to those gathered with this extended family. I once served with a pastor who often stated that "there is no sweeter fellowship than what evolves from serving together in the name of Jesus." The same could be said of the environment of worship that emanates from those preparing to serve through this ministry of the choir. I recall singing in the Oratorio Chorus during my days at Southern Baptist Theological Seminary in Louisville, Kentucky. A dear friend and member of the chorus was away tending to family responsibilities in relation to his father's critical illness. He was scheduled to be absent from a rehearsal, tending to his duties. During the evening's rehearsal of the Brahms *Requiem* taking place in the otherwise empty chapel at the seminary, my friend entered the room, slipping into a back pew. His presence we would later learn was due to the passing of his father. No official attention was given to his presence, nor was there any announcement at that time regarding his father's passing from this life. Even so, there seemed to be a unique and mysterious awareness among the singers who could see him seated just under the balcony in that sanctuary. As we sang "blessed are they who die in the Lord," there was a very strong sense of the Lord's presence with us and sense of ministry through God's holy Word to this Christian brother in that moment. Such occurrences of extended family worship speak in the moment when they happen and often lock themselves in our spiritual memories to resurface in other settings, reminding us of the holy presence of the Lord who meets with us whenever two or three are gathered in His name.

Congregational Worship

The worship gathering that is likely most-oft referenced and considered in discussions of worship is the gathering of the local church for congregational worship. Unlike the other worship groupings included in this chapter's discussions, examples of congregational worship can be seen from the first days of the church in the New Testament. Congregational worship is the grouping of worshipers for which most churches build and set aside an identifiable space, a sanctuary, that comes to signify worship and church itself, not only to those who attend, but to those in the community who drive by, no matter how infrequently. Challenges intrinsic to such gatherings can be seen from those first days, and continue to the present time. As we have already seen, the apostle Paul saw need to address issues within the congregation that arise from worship gatherings and admonishes believers regarding attitudes and practices of gathered worship. From the beginning of the New Testament church, it is apparent that the human condition presented similar problems in worship as were part of all life's relationships in daily living. It is likely that music in the early church was limited to congregational singing, but that practice was not without its challenges when "everyone has a hymn," as we see indicated in 1 Corinthians 14:26.

Of all the gatherings for worship, congregational worship quite likely presents the most challenges. The congregational gathering in most instances is weekly, intergenerational, inclusive of all the family groupings that make up the congregation, and inclusive of those who are brand new to the faith as well as those who have been part of the faith community long enough to be able to articulate its history in detail. On any Sunday, the gathering will include worshipers who may be experiencing deep hurt within their life circumstances, expecting church worship to be a place of lament and healing. Other worshipers will be "on top of the world," and anticipating a celebrative atmosphere to assist their own sense of well-being. Ecclesial understanding of what it means to be church sets the tone for how a congregation and its leaders will approach questions of gathered worship in general, and music for singing worship in particular.

We will discuss words and music for congregational worship settings in more detail in subsequent chapters. It is important in this consideration of worship groupings, however, to point out the complexity of bringing together the languages that worshipers might find meaningful in each setting. It would seem clear that the setting most ripe for intense collision of contrasting expectations is the congregational worship gathering. Ministers charged with the responsibility of selecting and leading songs in the congregational gathering need pastoral wisdom and strong theological foundation to guide such gatherings in a manner that helps worshipers genuinely "admonish one another with psalms, hymns, and spiritual songs" (Col 3:16).

Festival Worship

Throngs of college students flooded the streets surrounding the arena in downtown Nashville, all headed like ants to the opening sessions of Passion, a worship gathering that was to include Christian artist sensations Chris Tomlin and the Dave Crowder Band, as well as charismatic speakers

Louie Giglio and John Piper. Most of the individuals in the gathering crowd likely had church connections, either current or immediate past. Though networking took place in restaurants, hotels, and night spots around the downtown streets of Music City, it could be noted that many, if not most, of the connections being made were very much coincidental to the purpose that drew the students to attend this unique gathering of people from all across the U.S., Canada, and beyond. For many, that purpose included worship. If you could interview these young adults concerning their reason for attending such an event, you would likely hear the word *worship* a lot, mostly in terms of experience.

Inside the large arena built for hockey, country and rock music concerts, and other entertainment gatherings, the atmosphere is indistinguishable from a rock concert, with the marked exception that many of the attendees are carrying Bibles, wearing t-shirts with Scripture imprinted on them, and are entering the facility in a pleasant, orderly, even polite manner. The decibel level of the bands inside the arena and the energy from the stage are scaled down slightly from what a rock concert might bring, but not a whole lot. Over the course of the three-day event, the music varies from a hard rock feel to contemplative acoustic simplicity. The crowd is carried along with the mood and expression emanating from the platform throughout. Further analysis finds that music expressions stylized to be palatable to the age of the crowd actually have origins in everything from ancient psalm settings to revivalist era hymns to gospel music. Interestingly, the timbre of the speakers seems not much different from what would be expected in church settings.

I recall similarities to this environment from my first attendance at a Billy Graham crusade or the Promise Keepers rallies in stadiums that drew thousands of men across America. In each case, there was a celebrity status of platform personalities. At each event, it was likely that the vast majority of the attendees did not know each other, yet shared a common focus that prepared them for a high energy, high adrenaline rush that characterized such gatherings, and may have actually defined them after all was said and done. Though on a much smaller scale, some denominational convention gatherings and parachurch conferencing can produce similar festival environments. Syd Hielema reminds us that in such gatherings (for the most part), people who have gathered are strangers to each other, and thus have very little relational baggage. Participants know the celebrity leaders by reputation, adding to the expectancy and energy of the gathered crowd, thus affecting each attendee as well.

Festival worship gatherings are sometimes stamped by signature songs or music styles. Attendees expect to participate in singing these tunes as part of the experience, and often come away from the events with the music ringing in their ears and stuck in their head to the extent that hearing it reminds them of the gathering, and hopefully of personal commitments made there. Though feuds in churches over music styles often point to styles adopted from such events "invading" our church repertoire, the fact is that festival gatherings have influenced congregational worship liturgy for many years. Most Baptist churches reflect the liturgy flow of a Billy Graham crusade, having attended, observed on television, and even imitated the music and evangelistic preaching style of this successful organization led by a gifted gospel preacher.

Worship Repertoire in Different Gatherings

Each of the worship environments described—private worship, family worship, congregational worship, and festival worship—tends to have its own worship material repertoire. The music I sing in my time alone with God may include the new song that is still stewing in my mind and heart, but has not even been written down yet. I may sing my brokenness or specific personal confession and sing it in a very intimate manner in private worship. Family worship music expression probably includes very different material at a youth retreat than at a senior adult luncheon, yet the overall worship life of those involved in either of these settings is likely affected in the singing. Worship music sung in these settings adds to the repertoire (musical and otherwise) of the individual believer, and over time has effect on the repertoire of the whole church of which they are a part. The language and material of each separate setting in some way influences the other gatherings. For example, the festival worship environments often have profound influence on those who participate. The sound of hundreds or thousands of college students singing high energy praise can linger for a long time in our ears. Experiences that enliven our faith are often associated with such environments. Many a husband and father have made deep spiritual commitment in those stadiums where Promise Keepers' gatherings were accompanied by pounding drumbeats that marshaled the troops of God's army. Many high school and college musicians have deepened their faith while singing the music of master composers in massive gatherings of choristers who share a passion for music and utilize it as worship through expression of this art form. Just as effective in worshipers' lives may have been the intimate expressions that characterized a youth retreat, where coming to faith was emphasized and "best friends" openly shared thoughts and emotions connected by their faith.

It seems the most complex worship environment is intergenerational congregational worship. More than in any of the other environments, congregational worship gathers the expectations and aesthetical diversity of multiple generations. In this open setting, a glance across the room may remind worshipers of interactions that occurred outside the worship context. A young couple may spot the banker who is to blame for rejecting their loan application blocking the purchase of their first home. Singing in harmony as fellow believers may stretch the faith of both parties. A school teacher who questioned a student's fidelity on a test answer may struggle to receive the ministry of a youth praise team that includes the suspected offender. The worship leader who chose someone else's child as the lead role for the Christmas play may come across as offensive to the parents who are trying to find ways their little "angel" can fit in to the children's program. In other words, church can be messy. Tensions that are natural to communities of faith cannot really be "left at the door" of the sanctuary. Rather, they may be intensified and complicated in the setting where persons are being called upon to give themselves over to group music expression that presumes community. The tension is further perplexing when the music used seems more fitted to one age group than another. Worship wars, so-called, are not limited to contention over the material itself. Origins of such battles often stem from fear of losing something important to groups of worshipers. Awkwardness can abound when a group is being called upon to offer music from another generation or setting. Older adults may fear the loss of connection to the faith expressions they hope will be passed on to their grandchildren. Each unfamiliar song may intensify such feelings. Teenagers and young adults who want worship to feel comfortable and "relevant" to current life context may feel disconnected from the sounds and poetry of the music that appeals to their elders.

These repertoire additions can be healthy reminders of important experiences of worship for those who attended them. They can serve as spiritual markers of personal or group sense of the work of the Holy Spirit in a particular setting. A song often serves as an *Ebenezer* (marker of remembrance) that can remind us of the Lord's protection, intervention, unique visitation, or conviction from a previous experience in life.[6]

---

6 In the hymn, "Come, Thou Fount of Every Blessing," by Robert Robinson, stanza two begins with reference to the Ebenezer, which is a poetic reference to 1 Sam 7:12, "thus far has the Lord helped us."

A prominent source of confusion in worship singing takes place when expectations carry over from one type of worship gathering environment to the other. Worshipers who have been swept away in the festival worship gathering may expect the same energy level from their local church's congregational worship environment. Disappointment that the Sunday worship experience does not rise to the heightened emotional state of the festival environment may lead worshipers to experience ill feelings toward those they perceive as blocking such experience. The blaming may be pointed at the worship leader or other worshipers who "just don't get it." Having their expectations unmet may lower the degree of participation in the local church worship environment. This "festival envy syndrome" is not uncommon in our celebrity culture that values entertainment and service provision so highly.[7] Worshipers experiencing this "syndrome" may blame the song selection list, the worship leader, the pastor, or others in the congregation, forgetting that these were not present for the festival.

A youth group that has just returned from a time of awakening and intimate sharing may leave the next Sunday worship time wondering where those feelings were that characterized their experience from the family worship setting. On the other hand, a stately hymn that an intergenerational local church congregation sings with firm resolve and conviction may not translate well into a typical youth retreat setting, a festival setting, or a time of private worship.

It is true that expectations that are transferred from one worship environment to the other can lead to disappointment and can deter from a positive sense of community among gathered worshipers. A reality that cannot be overemphasized, however, is that each of the four contexts has a legitimate contribution that it makes to the worship life of the individual believer, and that each holds great potential to enhance the ongoing worship expression of the church worldwide, as well as the local church. Believers may discover connection and expression in one of the contexts that sensitizes them to the need for that connection in other environments, and fosters a new level of participation in all four contexts of worship gatherings.

More will be said about pastoral leadership and approach in worship leading in a later chapter. It should be stated here, however, that much can be accomplished through worship education to help worshipers to minister to one another in and through worship and worship singing, as

7 Syd Hielema, "The Festival-Envy Syndrome: Four Contexts of Worship" *Reformed Worship,* (March 2004), 3–5.

they are called to "speak to one another in psalms, hymns, and spiritual songs" (Col 3:16). Because worship expression encompasses all of life, when the community of faith comes together it brings all its experiences from outside the gathered body and, during gathered worship, participates in the ministry of mutuality.[8]

8 Stanley Grenz, *Theology for the Community of God* (Grand Rapids, MI: William B. Eerdmans, 2000), 492–501. Grenz discusses ways the church expresses its ministry of shared edification, which he describes as growing from its ecclesiology. Singing is one of the ways this mutuality is expressed.

Chapter 4
WORDS WE SING IN WORSHIP

The first time I traveled to Rio de Janeiro, I visited Campo Grande Church. My close worship pastor friend, Wayne Causey, and I were escorted by mission leaders to the meeting site of this large congregation. The building did not look particularly "churchy" from the outside, but people were streaming to the facility from all directions, and the relatively small parking lot immediately in front of the church was absolutely full of cars. Our escort informed us that most people walked to the church from the surrounding neighborhoods. Though still experiencing a bit of jet lag, I was excited to be worshiping in this church in another part of the world. As the service began, I was infatuated with the sounds of fellowship expressed in a different language.

I was not prepared for the emotional wave that came over me as the congregation began to sing songs of praise with high spirit and enthusiasm. There was something inexplicable about the sound of the Portuguese language expressed in community in a manner that sounded so passionate. Songs included tunes or forms that were familiar, even though I did not know the language. I was hoping they might sing "How Great Thou Art" since its refrain was about the only song I knew in Portuguese, but I found the familiar music of "Shout to the Lord" and "Praise to the Lord, the Almighty" to be tools for praise with which I could join in spirit even though I could not begin to even fake the Portuguese lyrics. I found my mind dancing back and forth between the excitement of hearing these newfound brothers and sisters in Christ sing in their native tongue, and mentally singing the English lyrics that I knew so well. Phrases like "shout to the Lord all the earth let us sing" meant much in this setting where I was made so aware that another part of the earth was alive with God's praise. My heart resonated with the hymn's instruction to "ponder anew what the Almighty can do," even though I had no idea which Portuguese phrase actually voiced that worship lyric.

Any study of worship singing obviously includes a study of the words used as well as the music that carries them. Each of these components, words and music, bears a portion of the load in our dialogue with God. One of my contentions is that in free church tradition, much of the work of the liturgy rests upon the shoulders of the singing, since no prescription *per se* has been mandated. Worship actions—confession, declaration of pardon, illumination, praise, passing of the peace—often are accomplished in these free church environments only as they are sung. Many volumes have been written regarding texts and music of worship songs. Pastors and theologians have pointed out that much of our theology is received and expressed through the songs we sing. As described in this chapter's opening illustration, there are times when we may not even know for certain the meaning of the words we sing in the moment we sing them, and yet it is not impossible in those moments to be engaged in the worship either through a sense of familiarity of music, environment, a memory association, or some other aspect of the worship in the moment. What's more, our words will never be "right" enough to make our worship worthy anyway. We are always wholly dependent upon Jesus, the true worship leader and our High Priest, for that.

If we know who is singing or saying the words of worship and have some sense of the level of their engagement, we may be able to know more of the controlling point of the worship. In systems where words of liturgy are not understood to hold some mystical power in themselves, they *are* expected to reflect the power of the gospel, the power of worship. The repetition, or "re-oralizing" of Scripture, song, sermon, words of institution, blessing, and other worship material within the context of culture, history, and church reflect the ethos of the church.[1] As moral response among

1 Russell F. Mitman, *Worship in the Shape of Scripture* (Cleveland: The Pilgrim Press, 2001), 130–132.

believers, "Worship awakens a vision of their commonality, which in turn awakens their concern for justice, for one another, and for the wholeness of the community."[2]

The aspect of the worship service for evangelicals that most often invites people to articulate the words of their worship is congregational singing. While an occasional responsive reading or group prayer recitation may be used in some church environments, most, if not all, churches provide opportunity for singing in every service of gathered worship. Much can be known about a congregation's worship, doctrine, mission, and ethos through a careful reflection upon the songs that are used in gathered worship. I invite you to consider three functions of the singing, paying special attention to what words are sung and how they are sung in the local church environment. We will consider how worship singing assists spiritual formation, how worship singing expresses ministry among the worshiping community itself, and then consider how worship singing deals with worship tensions.

Spiritual Formation and Singing

The words we speak or sing and the piety within which we speak them in worship give us means of study regarding the controlling point of worship. The words reflect what we believe, and continue to form what we believe. The historic motto, *lex orandi, lex credendi*, word/rule/law of prayer is the word/rule/law of belief, "asserts that our prayer not only expresses our faith, but that it also forms our theology."[3] As Robert Wilken states,

> The faith is embedded in language. It is not a set of abstract beliefs or ideas, but a world of shared associations and allusions with its own beauty sonority, inner cohesion and logic, emotional and rhetorical power. The Church's way of speaking is a collection of the words and images that have formed the thinking and actions of those who have known Christ.[4]

2 Carol Doran and Thomas H. Troeger, *Trouble at the Table: Gathering the Tribes for Worship* (Nashville: Abingdon Press, 1992), 39.

3 Paul Richardson, "Spiritual Formation in Christian Worship," *Review & Expositor,* 96 (1999), 519.

4 Robert Wilken, "The Church's Way of Speaking," *First Things: A Monthly Journal of Religious and Public Life,* Issue 155, August/September, 2005, 29.

One of the ways worship is formative is through instruction that is part of its language. Worshipers expect worship to include instruction for their faith. Preachers do well to take on the task of instruction and to recognize the need for assisting worshipers in application of biblical knowledge. After all, our faith includes a vast range of concepts. The most obvious worship element that conveys instruction is the sermon, or preaching. Unfortunately, in many instances, preaching has come to be understood as the only instructive aspect of worship. Very frequently I hear leaders use language that somehow divides "worship" (as reference to music expression) from "preaching" (a reference to the pastor's teaching or sermon). Such dichotomy is misleading on both sides of the equation in that it seems to rob preaching of its place of centrality to what worship is all about (an engagement with God), and it robs music and singing of its instructive quality. Such a division, which I believe characterizes much of our modern evangelical worship, skews worshipers' participation in mutuality. They may miss out on the giving and receiving that occurs in the ministry of singing that fosters ministry, community building, and admonition. Debra and Ron Rienstra state it well: "Since *everything* spoken or sung in worship has an inherently formative dimension, not just the obviously instructive words, to call only one part of the service 'teaching' is misleading."[5] Indeed, words of song can instruct us in our worship, as in "O worship the King, all glorious above; and gratefully sing His wonderful love." Singing can instruct our life practice of daily disciplines, such as in, "Take time to be holy, speak oft with Thy Lord," or it can remind us to bear our witness as in "Share His love by telling what the Lord has done for you."[6] We could go on to include songs that instruct in nearly every aspect of Christian living.

Another way worship and worship singing is formative is through prayer. Much of our worship singing is prayer that directly addresses God. Worshipers sing words of praise, lament, confession, cries for help, and proclamation to God in sung prayers. Singing our thanks in prayer to God helps form us to be grateful people. It helps us to be expectant when we have prayed our testimony to God that "morning by morning new mercies I see."[7] Here again, singing these prayers serves to form the worshipers that express them.

Precisely because of the formative value of the words of our worship singing, it is crucial that worship planners exercise discernment and

5 Debra and Ron Rienstra, *Worship Words: Discipling Language for Faithful Ministry* (Grand Rapids, MI: Baker Academic, 2009) 35.

6 See topical index of hymnals or worship songbooks. Worship planning aids such as the *Resource and Planning Edition Baptist Hymnal and Worship Hymnal* (Nashville: Lifeway Worship, 2009).

7 Thomas Chisholm, "Great Is Thy Faithfulness" in *Baptist Hymnal 2008*, #96.

discretion in selecting material. In our day of unprecedented proliferation of songs aimed at the "worship market," theologically weak lyrics can find their way into the worship language of churches. Rather than pick at individual songs, I would point readers to work done by Lester Ruth in analyzing the top seventy-seven songs by use between 1989 and 2005 as indicated by Christian Copyright Licensing, Inc. (CCLI).[8] The songs' lyrics were analyzed for Trinitarian address, content, and function. He discovered very little attention to this matter and makes clear observations relative to the lack of such focus. This is especially alarming for evangelicals in general and Baptists in particular, as primary users of these materials. The most recent publication of *The Baptist Hymnal*, as well as many other recently published song collections, includes most of these titles, an indication of the popularity of their use much more than the quality of their theological value for spiritual formation.[9]

The classic understanding *lex orandi, lex credeli,* the rule of praying is the rule of believing, is replaced in the words of these songs by a completely different focus. This emphasis is *lex amandi, lex orandi,* that is, the rule of loving establishes the rule of praying. In response, Ruth points to the piety engendered in these songs: "The One worshiped is someone whom we love and enjoy and Who is with us, but there is little sense of Christians being brought into the activity of this God, particularly if this God whom we worship is conceived of as a Triune community."[10] Almost all of these songs describe the dynamic between worshipers and the Divine recipient of worship, not the relationship and activity—past, present, and future—among the Persons of the Trinity." The piety of the singing of these words coincides with the words themselves. Many worship leaders have adapted

8 Lester Ruth "How Great Is Our God: The Trinity in Contemporary Christian Worship Music" in *The Message in the Music: Studying Contemporary Praise & Worship* (Nashville: Abingdon Press, 2009), 13–42. The introduction to the book provides a detail description of the means by which the song list of seventy-seven songs was obtained. Ruth describes a five-question test by which he analyzed the lyrics of each song.

9 The Baptist Hymnal published by Lifeway Worship includes seventy-four of the seventy-seven titles in its printed hymnal. Inclusion is not surprising given the philosophical starting point of this project. Lifeway Worship Director, Mike Harland, said the new hardbound hymnal is being planned with a new mentality. "In other hymnals, we've had the mentality of publishing what planners thought the churches ought to sing. In this selection process, we are engaging hundreds of music leaders and asking, 'what are the churches singing?' and we'll make selections from there ... The new hymnal will include old favorite hymns as well as new favorites and choruses." Reported in *Facts & Trends* (Nashville: Lifeway, December 4, 2006).

10 Lester Ruth, "How Great Is Our God: The Trinity in Contemporary Christian Music" in *The Message in the Music* (Nashville: Abingdon Press, 2009), 36.

some form of the teaching that uses the physical structure of the Temple of the Old Testament to serve as a model of the spiritual "flow" desirable through worship singing. In such "flow," the worshipers move from the outer courts of thanksgiving along the path of praise, and finally to the acute intimacy within the Holy of Holies, where the deepest passions of the worshiper can be expressed. This worship piety often differentiates between "praise" and "worship" with the latter representing a much closer sense of intimate adoration.[11]

Such piety is fitting and consistent within charismatic church traditions, where music is understood as sacrament. An objective within this framework is personal intimacy and immediacy of the Holy Spirit, which is achieved largely through the singing. Ruth states, "A more classic approach is to make God's activity on our behalf-from the Father through the Son in the Spirit—mirrored in the response of worship—in the Spirit through the Son to the Father. Thus the classic approach, in contrast to the tendency of these songs, puts the emphasis on God's graciousness from first to last. The classic approach keeps Jesus as "lead worshiper" within the internal love of the Trinity."[12]

Spiritual formation follows the direction of our expressions through our prayer singing.

Singing Words that Form Community

Through my years of leading and participating in worship music in local congregations, I have had the marvelous privilege of having observed community formed in worship singing. A unique interaction occurs as the words of hymns and worship songs are sung. The interaction occurs not only among the singers and God, who is the object of our worship, but also between the words and the people singing them. The people are forming the words, and the words are forming the people. Sometimes the words reflect who these people are, and that reflection begins to speak to the meaning of the words themselves.

Sheldon C. Coleman was the CEO of his family business, The Coleman Company of Wichita, Kansas (as in Coleman lanterns and stoves). This

---

11 Barry Liesch, *The New Worship: Straight Talk on Music and the Church* (Grand Rapids, MI: Baker Books, 1996) 61–70. Liesch provides a deliberate and respectful description of the phases of this worship piety especially referencing the work of charismatic Judson Cornwall.

12 Lester Ruth, "How Great Is Our God: The Trinity in Contemporary Worship Music" in *The Message in the Music* (Nashville: Abingdon Press, 2009), 36.

entrepreneurial giant was a powerful force in the business world, yet his Christian faith characterized his life and drove his humble spirit. It was my privilege to serve as music minister for Metropolitan Baptist Church in Wichita, where Sheldon Coleman was a member. On the Sundays he was not traveling the world with his business concerns, he could be found on the fourth row, organ side of the sanctuary of the church, enthusiastically singing the hymns on the same row as the night janitor who worked in his Fortune 500 company. Coleman loved music, loved to sing, and was a dependable passionate participant in Sunday worship hymn singing. One of the legends for which Coleman was known was that he personally tried every product his company manufactured. My one-time visit to his office confirmed the legend in my mind, as photographs and trinkets that demonstrated his love for the outdoors were among the things he wanted to discuss. It was fitting that at his funeral service the congregation sang "This Is My Father's World," a reminder that creation ultimately belongs to its Creator. Equally moving to me as I led that congregational song at the memorial service was the sight of the night janitor joining heartedly in the singing. Having been acquainted with such a well-known figure left a bold impression on me. The most lasting aspect of that memory, however, is the sight of Mr. Coleman singing on Sundays as part of that congregation he loved.

Marva Dawn reminds us, "We don't go to church, we *are* the church and go to worship to learn how to be the church."[13] As one who leads worship music, I sometimes find myself trying to "create" community when the fact is that community already exists. Dr. Constance Cherry reminds us, "Christian community is already a divine reality. Community is not something which can be created. It can only be expressed."[14] It is as a church that these people gather "to work out their problems in the one context, to set their needs within the framework of one community … the community of faith."[15] Brian Wren says, "In the act of singing, the members not only support one another, but proclaim a community of faith reaching beyond

13 Marva Dawn, *A Royal Waste of Time: The Splendor of Worshiping God and Being Church for the World* (Grand Rapids, MI: Eerdmans Publishing, 1999), 256–257.

14 Constance Cherry, "Convergence Worship—A Matter of Community," in *Creator Magazine,* May/June, 1999, 27.

15 William Willimon, *Worship as Pastoral Care,* 41. Willimon presents the arguments of Paul Pruyser of the Menninger Foundation, particularly related to why people seek psychotherapy within the faith community as opposed to other environments, as presented in *The Journal of Pastoral Care,* Vol. 31 (March, 1977), 23–31.

the congregation that sings."[16] Our singing has a way of connecting us to the church that has sung these songs before and to those who sing worship round the world. Songs that confront injustice and awaken our senses to the presence of God in the world (incarnational) should move us in the direction Christ gave in the Great Commission (Matt 28:19–20). Worship together is central to what it means to be a community of faith, but it also compels us to act in ways the church has been commissioned to act. Singing helps us remember. Anamnesis not only recalls the past, but restores the past to make it part of the present. "This practice of remembering helps form us into a people who know their place in history, a people of both humility and great hope."[17]

Congregational song reflects the communal nature of our worship and our oneness in Christ. The act of such singing serves to sensitize us to the ministry needs and concerns of those in our midst as well as to others for whom we as congregation need to play our role as a royal priesthood; a bridge between God's truth and hard realities of life. "Worship helps people not to escape life, but to face it."[18] Singing within a sense of community offers fellow believers a priestly role to one another as they voice ministry, confrontation, encouragement, and mutual edification through the words of their singing. Singing plays an important role in forming community not only with song lyrics that provide declaration of community, such as "We are One in the Bond of Love," or "Undivided," but also through words that simply utilize collective pronouns as mutual expression. The mutuality of ministry during congregational singing is a feature of its mystery. A matrix of ministry occurs as worshipers sing admonition to one another, thus they are giving and receiving ministry at once, its application made to those ministry needs known to the present Holy Spirit. Community formation is served through the use of "we" songs. A careful review of many churches' song lists should remind us that we need more "we" songs.

What it means to be *church* affects the position and expression of corporate worship for any congregation. J. I. Packer notes that "Roman Catholic, Orthodox, high Anglicans and leading ecumenists often say that evangelicals have an inadequate view of the church. Is that true? In theory, no, but in practice the answer often appears to be yes."[19] Baptist worship

---

16 Brian Wren, *Praying Twice,* 93.

17 Debra and Ron Rienstra, *Worship Words: Discipling Language for Faithful Ministry* (Grand Rapids, MI: Baker Books, 2009), 39.

18 William Willimon, Ibid., 100.

19 J. I. Packer, *Ancient & Postmodern Christianity,* 124

is of the free church tradition, and as such has continued to be directed by pastors and worship music leaders who have made the decisions of what worship material will be included in weekly worship practice. Since Baptist ecclesiology is non-connectional, factors of evangelistic fervor, revivalist practice, and church growth models in this century have placed church leaders in a position of decision-making that is "result-oriented," and this pragmatism has had great impact upon the manner and means of worship ethos in the local church. In the broader evangelical community, the individualistic culture seems to have driven corporate worship to reflect a private expression as a group of individual worshipers, rather than as the bride of Christ. In a highly individualistic and over-stimulated culture, it is of little wonder that corporate worship allowed to do so would drift toward this individualized expression. Packer expresses concern over what has been lost in this individualization:

> The church then comes to be thought of as an organization for spiritual life support rather than as an organism of perpetual praise; doxology is subordinated to ministry, rather than ministry embodying and expressing doxology; ... church life is thought of as furthering people's salvation rather than of worshiping and glorifying God.[20]

Words of worship are most evident in the songs we sing. If word expressions used in corporate worship are purposely personal in their expression, even exclusive of other relationships or sense of community, those words contribute to the individualistic ethos that may well reflect an anthropocentric tendency. The Frontier Revival movement in America can be credited to a large extent for a move toward personalized worship expression within the gathered worship setting. Reflecting on this change, David Dockery notes, "The movement from subtlety and dignity to freedom and straightforwardness also resulted in services characterized by a shift toward a more anthropocentric emphasis. The main purpose of the service was defined in terms of what *happened to people* rather than what was *offered to God.*"[21]

---

20 J.I. Packer, *Ancient & Postmodern Christianity,* 125.

21 David Dockery, *Southern Baptist Consensus and Renewal: A Biblical, Historical, and Theological Proposal* (Nashville: Broadman & Holman, 2008), 106–117. Dockery presents a well-documented, concise history of Baptist worship noting the major streams of Baptist expressions and following their merge into Baptist distinctives.

In a culture obsessed with self, the church that is true to Scripture offers a counter message that values community and encourages the individual's participation within that community as expression of worship not only within the community itself, but as an integrated whole expressing its praise to God. There is a glaring need within the evangelical community, including Baptists, for singing that forms and expresses community. "Baptists have agreed with the Reformers that the unity of the church is spiritual, not organizational or institutional." Indeed, "as there is unity in the Godhead, so there is unity in his church."[22] Congregationalist governance itself is based on this principle. High frequency of individualistic worship expression, such as demonstrated in much of our songs, and low frequency of corporate and missional expression as "priesthood of the believers," would seem to foster non-relational worship. If the interrelatedness of the Triune nature of God and the corporate nature of worship expression is not being fostered, and the conjoined spirit of the church, "visible and invisible," is not characteristic of worship language, one wonders how worship can possibly be theocentric.

Tensions of Worship

The word *tension* conjures up negative connotations for most of us when contemplated in the context of the worship environment of the local church. As one who consults often with churches on worship matters, I am called upon to help churches negotiate stresses that arise from differences within the congregation regarding such issues. These consultations often center on stylistic preferences, which certainly can be the source of tensions, some of which are unhealthy. The fact of the matter, however, is that where there is life, there *is* tension. Authentic Christian worship has life, and authentic worship includes tensions. In fact, worship of a holy God in a fallen world is at its core full of tension. Worship singing provides a viable means of presenting, negotiating, and even celebrating these tensions. Although style issues certainly can introduce pressures, I want to consider more primary worship matters. One example of such a tension in worship is the conflict that is a subplot, so to speak, of this very book's matter. I am referring to the *tension between individual and congregational worship*. In Baptist theology, this is a healthy contradiction, as Baptists understand a personal relationship with God in Christ to be a foundation for what

22 John S. Hammett, *Biblical Foundations for Baptist Churches: A Contemporary Ecclesiology* (Grand Rapids: Kregel Academic and Professional, 2005), 54.

it means to be Christian, but also understand that the individual who is truly a part of the faith will become an integral part of a local church body. Worship words expressed through singing gives us opportunity to sing our personal worship as part of community, and at once allows communal worship as individual Christ-followers. Though at tension with one another, these two aspects of worship assist one another and thus, the worshipers they engage. In a later chapter, I will address singing and sacred actions in worship, such as the ordinances of baptism and the Lord's Supper, in which these tensions are heightened and celebrated simultaneously to God's glory.

A beloved pastor was leaving his church in Atlanta to become part of a denominational staff in another state. The church gathered for the final service before his departure. There was a palpable energy among those gathered for the emotional celebration that marked the end of an era. Memories of the nine years under the pastor's leadership were reviewed and shared. Amid tears and occasional outbursts of applause and laughter, the service was closed with singing the great prayer and praise hymn, "Great Is Thy Faithfulness." Some church members reflected on moments the pastor and his wife had stood with them at the crib of a new baby, the hospital bed of a dying parent, or at the altar of wedding. Their worship expressed praise for God's faithfulness as they sang, "morning by morning new mercies I see." At once, there was a realization of spiritual and communal growth that had taken place within this community of faith over the pastor's tenure. The singing was robust and gloriously unified at each refrain that proclaimed "great is Thy faithfulness." Singing gave worshipers opportunity of expression within both individual and corporate meaning at once in their celebrative singing. Our present day context of an individualistic culture and a church practice that has drifted to an imbalance to the individual piety within the corporate expression may call for a corrective. Paul Richardson is correct in stating, "Though there is certainly a relationship between corporate worship and individual spiritual formation, our greater need is to be formed as the Body of Christ, the very thing that corporate Christian worship uniquely does."[23] When worship language is highly personalized, this unity formation may be thwarted. Therefore, in popular practice, what happens in corporate worship is that

23 Lester Ruth, "*Lex Amandi, Lex Orandi*: The Trinity in the Most Used Contemporary Christian Worship Songs," Prepared for and delivered at a conference entitled "The Place of Christ in Liturgical Prayer: Christology, Trinity, and Liturgical Theology," Yale Institute of Sacred Music, February 27, 2005.

"grace, reconciliation, shared faith, tradition, a sense of the transcendent all have bowed to people's immediate concerns and experience."[24]

Historic Baptist worship centers in the Word of God. As already noted, all worship words must be in keeping with biblical authority. How we approach God is to be governed by Scripture, a theological approach known as the *Regulative Principle.*[25] If worship is to be truly "about God" and not "about us," then we must be careful to shape our worship in Who God is in Christ, and the Word of God is the fully reliable source of that revelation. The tensions of God's character expressed by singing lyrics that are true to biblical revelation combine with preaching, reading, and praying to help us worship "in spirit and truth." (John 4:24) While some interpret this inference to be about us, whereby "spirit" has to do with our sincerity, and "truth" connotes our heartfelt intentions, I would contend with Mark Dever, among others, that "the Spirit referred to is not our spirit, but the Holy Spirit. He is called the Spirit of truth several times in John (14:17; 15:26; 16:13). And the truth is also a reference to God, even to Jesus Himself, who said that He is the truth" (John 14:16).[26]

In worship, there is tension between the reality of God's divine transcendence and His divine immanence. Worship singing gives us means of singing this tension without excluding either characteristic of God. We can hold them with equal amazement. He is "Immortal, Invisible, God only wise." He is at once the one who has called us friend, toward whom we sing "I Am a Friend of God." God is wholly other, yet is also closer than a brother. Singing allows us to hold this tension in our worship through the words of the songs we sing. It is part of the mystery that engages our faith. In worship, a similar tension presents *God's familiarity with His mystery.* Singing helps us revere the "splendour of the King robed in majesty,"[27] while at once recognizing "there is a place of quiet rest near to the heart of God."[28]

---

24 Carol Doran and Thomas Troeger, "Reclaiming the Corporate Self" in *Worship 60.03,* 202.

25 The Regulative Principle of worship teaches that only those elements instituted by command, precept, or example of Scripture are permitted in worship. It is often contrasted to the Normative Principle, which teaches that whatever is not prohibited in Scripture is permissible in public worship practice as long as it is agreeable and encourages unity in the church.

26 Michael Lawrence and Mike Dever, "Blended Worship" in *Perspectives on Christian Worship: 5 Views* (Nashville: B&H Academic, 2009), 229.

27 "How Great Is Our God" by Chris Tomlin in *Baptist Hymnal,* 5.

28 "Near to the Heart of God" by Cleland McAfee in *Baptist Hymnal,* 458.

Dynamics within the worship environment and elements themselves present tensions in worship embraced by singing. *Vertical emphasis verses horizontal emphasis* presents a tension that singing itself addresses by the directions of its own words. *Tradition verses innovation* is a tension in worship that stems not only from style issues, but seems inherent in biblical affinity rooted in Jewish heritage and orderliness, yet free in its expression "as the Spirit moves." Singing within these directions can press these tensions together, and may also address external tensions such as *formality verses casualness,* and even the tension of *participation verses mediation,* as the historic work of leadership through prophetic and priestly functions may be sung as well as expressed through other means in the worship act. Other tensions include *sacred place verses diaspora, sacred time verses ordinary time,* as in the very act of gathering on Sunday while singing of our service "every moment of every day."[29]

To help us better understand the interplay of the tensions of worship, it seems important that we consider more than the contemporary culture within which the church worships. Surely the well-versed pastor and worship music leader is aided by better understanding past paradigms and the church's language of worship within those contexts to consider the impact of cultural surroundings on ethos and piety in worship. Robert Webber has pointed out the advantage of looking at the church in this manner: "Paradigm thinking sets us free to affirm the whole church in all its previous manifestations."[30] Likewise, it seems logical that through such historic understanding, imbalances might be avoided and appropriate tensions might be held in proper convergence in our worship, including our singing.

Worship theologian John Witvliet confronts us with the fact: "As worship leaders, we have the important and terrifying task of placing words of prayer on people's lips. It happens every time we choose a song and write a prayer." [31] The selection of material scripturally sound, appropriate, attainable, singable, and generally usable within the language of the congregation is further complicated by its need to function at multiple levels. Again, though complicated, this is a part of the miracle and mystery of corporate worship. Brian Wren reminds us of a question to be asked in worship material selection: "Can people of different generations, cultures,

29 "Share His Love" by William J. Reynolds in *Baptist Hymnal,* 358.

30 Robert Webber, *Ancient Future Faith* (Grand Rapids: Baker Books, 1999), 16.

31 Witvliet, *Worship Seeking Understanding,* 282.

and circumstances find themselves in these words?"[32] I would ask more pointedly, "Can these different generations, cultures, and circumstances find the Lord in these words?"

Although Baptists are not known for recording the language of their worship, worship bulletins and/or "orders of service" give us some indication of material and direction of this worship, especially of congregational music.[33] A Mark Noll essay points out, "We are what we sing."[34] For years, many Baptists worshiped using regional language of song and later used denominational compilations, such as *The Baptist Hymnal.* In more recent days, diverse styles from a myriad of sources have contributed to the dissolution of common worship-speak among these churches, which may itself indicate anthropocentric tendencies. Study of worship orders among Baptist churches seems to indicate a certain lack of Baptist distinctive and identity.

As David S. Dockery points out, "much of Baptist worship tends: (1) to be confused about the purpose and order of worship; (2) to evidence a minimal use of the Bible, especially its public reading; (3) to be passive; and (4) to have an inadequate view of the church ordinances."[35]

Efforts to bring about correctives for such inadequacies in worship will surely include a close ongoing review of the words we sing.

---

32 Wren, *Praying Twice,* 184.

33 Not only are Baptists of the free church tradition, but frequently display a certain independent spirit that resists set worship orders, and by inference common books of worship prayers, or prescribed liturgy. Some have said the Baptist tradition is that of no tradition, although we would argue that Baptist worship tends to follow a predictable format with minimal variance following an understood prescription of its own tradition, or in present day practice, that adapted from some perceived "successful" other church of similar stylistic character. For further understanding of this process, particularly in recent Baptist life, see Terry York's, *American Worship Wars,* (Peabody, MA: Hendrickson Publishers, 2003), 20, 27, 47, 78–79, 84, 95, 102.

34 D. A. Carson, *Worship by the Book,* 32, noting the title of an essay by Noll in *Christianity Today,* 12 July, 1999, 37–41.

35 David S. Dockery, "Worship" in *Baptists Why and Why Not Revisited,* edited by Timothy and Denise George, (Nashville: Broadman and Holman, 1997), 135.

Chapter 5

MUSIC WE SING IN WORSHIP

Meaning in Music

During a consultation process with a church, I had asked participants to engage in an exercise aimed at helping them to understand how important music genres could be to those who were part of different age groups. The activity is geared to help church members come to grips with how strong emotions can become when we talk about music that is part of our faith expression. The exercise is designed on the presumption that believers care for one another enough to respect feelings and have some sense of how to treat one another Christianly. In leading the activity, I try to keep the atmosphere as lighthearted as possible. I was reading a list of examples of musical styles and mentioned rap music. I was startled when an elderly gentleman raised loud objection in a near shout, "Rap is not music!" My first inclination was to just ignore the outburst and move on to my point. I changed my mind when I heard the rumble from the teenagers in the back of the room. Attempting to keep the younger set engaged, since that was a huge reason I had been called into the setting in the first place, I invited a more specific open response. Looking to the back rows, I asked, "Do you guys like rap music?"

Oops! I had just said it again. The gentleman was sticking with his claim. He spoke up again, with an even more intense gruffness in his vocal inflection, "Rap is not music!" He even added, "Rap is crap!" Ouch!

What had I done? Asking that the man hold his comments until later, my mind was thinking, "Houston, we have a problem." I turned once again to the teens, who were now sending mixed signals, some indicating overt anger, others laughing, and still others cowing down as if defeated by the process. I felt I needed to try to hold them in the conversation. I asked again, "Do you guys like rap?"

After an awkward silence and a couple of repetitions of the question, a young man offered, "I do! Rap is great." Some of the teens giggled and others looked a bit embarrassed. Within a few seconds, they were talking among themselves, and adults in the room appeared nervous. I followed up asking, "What is it about rap that you like?"

One of the teenage girls spoke up. "I like rap ok … I like the beat … but I don't think we should use rap music in church." I was disappointed with my facilitation skills, as I had broken my first rule of worship dialogue, which is "we are not here to talk about what any of us like, or do not like."

Eventually the discussion and the whole consultation found more common ground for healthy conversation and interchange. Care was expressed and worship language in the church's worship was adjusted slightly to be a bit more inclusive, while remaining respectful to its history and to all of its members.

I came away from that exchange with an important question on my mind. What *is* music? How can I give some helpful definition that lay persons and non-musicians can understand, since it is the art form of worship practice that is most referenced in Scripture and most consistently practiced in churches? I spend most of my waking hours talking about, listening to, and making music. I have never had anyone call to ask me, "Now, what exactly is music?" It seems to be a given that we all know what we are talking about when we address the subject. Most non-musicians have little interest in a detailed description of musical elements such as pitch, harmony, rhythm, tempo, timbre, or contour, much less meter, key, melody shape, loudness, form, or reverberation. In fact, musicians seem to have a language all our own. Even so, I am always amazed at how readily and confidently non-musicians in churches declare some music to be "good" or "bad." Such willingness undoubtedly stems from how saturated our culture is with music. Whether we know it or not, music is affecting us at the store, the movies, in our homes, work, and school. The old adage is probably true: "people know what they like, and like what they know." The discussion of whether or not rap music really is music is just that, a discussion. I am not seeking to address the rap genre as a worship tool at all here, but to use this consultation experience to call attention to the need to break down music components and application to their simplest form to help people consider how music is speaking to us and how carefully we might want to approach its usage as worship. Surely members of Christian community can and should converse extensively regarding the efficacy and appropriateness of music of varying styles in their context of worship, giving prayerful consideration to the teaching of Scripture and need of the faith community. Worship music leaders and pastors would seem to do well to encourage and facilitate such discussion, rather than avoiding it, as is often the case. It would seem that such conversations would hold great potential for believers to practice "doing nothing out of selfish ambition, or vain conceit, but in humility thinking of others as better than yourselves" (Phil 2:3–4). It would seem that such dialogue could allow the elements of music's effect to be assessed for their value, or lack thereof, for advancing engagement of community and individuals with a Holy God. I am often amazed at how scant attention is given to the character of music used in worship.

It is important to understand music as an art. Interestingly, the last twenty years have produced much discussion about worship and the arts. Quite often, however, conference topics and subject matter demonstrate a default setting whereby worship and the arts tends to mean painting, literature, drama, dance, and even film. Music is likely left from the listing because it is an understood aspect of Christian worship, given its biblical prominence compared to other art forms. Nevertheless, a careful study of its practice and effect seem to be appropriate arenas for theological address. There is not nearly enough space for such address in this volume, but readers are encouraged to give such consideration as part and parcel of what it means to prepare to lead congregations in worship through music and to engage them in congregational singing.

Obviously, discussion of congregational singing in worship includes discussion of music itself. Though I call this obvious, it has been my experience that Jeremy Begbie is correct when he points out, "the pitfall of turning all talk about music into talk about words."[1] Church leaders have a strong tendency to switch subjects as if talking about one completes the discussion of the other. This tendency is possibly the chief contributor to the lack of intelligible conversation between musicians and theologians for so long. I contend we need to rethink music less as an object in worship and more as an action. Christopher Small says we should think of it as "musicking" rather than "music."[2] Singing our worship as a gathered body of Christ indicates we are engaged in music-making and music-hearing. In the ministry setting of worship, it implies we are giving and receiving in the same action at the same time, and that in the presence of, and we trust in the power of, the Holy Spirit. It seems only appropriate then to consider not only the words we sing, but the function and appropriateness of the music we sing as well. Simple demonstrations of extremes can help congregations at least understand the most basic fundamentals of music's emotive powers and mechanics. Minor and major keys are often quickly identified by listeners as being "sad" or "happy," respectively. Matching a serious minor key tune or treatment with a lighthearted or uplifting lyric, or with a non-contemplative worship action, can demonstrate the way that music has an appropriateness component. This consideration goes a little deeper than the lyric-tune mismatches that overextend a tune's associations attached from other textual associations. Who of us has not heard (or sung) the lyric of "Amazing Grace, How Sweet the Sound" to the tune of "House of the Rising Sun"? (Yes, I am a child of the 60s.) Frank Burch Brown has a ridiculous setting of the pastoral 23rd psalm to be sung to the tune of "Rudolph the Red-nosed Reindeer."[3] The value of such extremes in demonstration is to help us go further to show what minimal adjustments in music have broader applications and associations. It can be beneficial for lay persons to recognize how much a slight change in some aspect of music can rob it of its impact or shift its emphasis. This is especially important in our day when so many historic hymns are being rearranged to reflect an updated harmonization and rhythmic vitality. Such changes may work with some songs better than others, but will always make some change in the perception and experience of the music itself, and by extension, the worship expression it seeks to support.

Music in worship elicits emotional response of various kinds. "Any discussion of the emotional response to music is faced at the very outset with the fact that very little is known about this response and its relation to the

1 Jeremy Begbie, *Resounding Truth* (Grand Rapids, MI: Baker Academic, 2007), 21–25.

2 Christopher Small, *Music of the Common Tongue: Survival and Celebration in Afro-American Music* (London: J. Calder, 1987), 50–52.

3 Frank Burch Brown "Mismatch" in *Christian Century* (March 2009), 23.

stimulus."[4] Evidence that it exists is based on testimony, introspective reports of composers, performers, and listeners. That music evokes emotion seems to be accepted, there is just not evidence that clearly says why. Even so, the effect is often profound, while at the same time complex and unpredictable. For example, different overt responses may mean the same thing … tears can indicate elation or sorrow … agitation or stillness can either indicate disdain or discomfort. Leonard Meyer indicates, "… what can be observed is not the emotion-felt, the affect, but only its adjuncts and concomitants, which in the case of behavior tend to become standardized and in the case of physiological changes are not specific to emotion."[5]

Different schools of thought attempt to define where music finds its meaning center. Absolutists take the position that music's meaning is within its own constructs. To them, music simply means itself. Referentialists see music as meaning something to which it refers, or in a way that is relative to something outside itself. The connective link, albeit an arbitrary connection, is assigned to symbol. Expressionists see meaning as coming in the music, but recognize that it may express something non-musical, tangible or otherwise. This is different than the referential meaning, which "may mean that in listening to a piece of music we experience the feelings we had when hearing the piece in the past." In addition, referential is not only personal, but also has to do with culture, which "suggests that musical meaning is contextual: music cannot be separated from its relationship to, and role in, society."[6]

The realities of music's impact and the development of preference patterns for music are apparently in direct relation to the amount of exposure in early life experiences, or at least such experiences may give indication as to what preferences might develop. Daniel Levitin tells of experiments that indicate responses from toddlers reflecting experiences from experimentation executed during their time in their mother's womb. The responses indicate a connection to types of music to which the infant was exposed even before birth.[7] Deeper understanding of such scientific discoveries may serve stylistic considerations

4 Leonard M. Meyer, *Emotion and Meaning in Music,* (Chicago: University of Chicago Publishing, 1956), 12.

5 Ibid., 12.

6 Mercedes Pavlicevic, *Music Therapy in Context: Music, Meaning and Relationship,* (London: Jessica Kingsley Publishers Ltd, 1997, second printing 2000), 21.

7 Daniel Levitin, *This Is Your Brain on Music: The Science of Human Obsession* (New York: Plume Publishing, 2006), Levitin is referring to experimentation that has been conducted since the 1960's and considers the so-called "Mozart effect" whereby children's intelligence is thought to be enhanced by listening to Mozart compositions in the womb and in the earliest days of human life. The discussion includes thoughts on ways music's preferences are developed. 223–246.

when aligned with consideration of the diversity of ethnicity and exposure included among the people of our individual congregations.

The music minister must face with some understanding the potential these complexities represent in address to the culture of the local church in general, but also in the sensitivities indicated by complexities of pastoral care needs and concerns in particular. Even so, as Don and Emily Saliers remind us, "ordered sound plays a primary role in human experiences, especially those we call religious or spiritual."[8] Frank Burch Brown states it this way, "Discernment in Christian music means going beyond just the words, important as those may be, and giving due consideration to music's own ways of being religious."[9] While our concern here is restricted to congregational music, it should be mentioned that all music within the public worship setting has a way of communicating meaning, and as such needs careful scrutiny and wise pastoral address. The best comparison I can make is to think of how language strikes the ear of a church member, or non-member for that matter, in the midst of a particular ministry need or condition. Imagine if a congregant had just lost a loved one to a battled disease, and a pastor walked into the visitor's waiting room at the hospital and used coarse language to tell a joke or even to inquire as to what happened in the loved one's death or doctors' response. Such insensitivity would be unconscionable in pastoral etiquette. The same sort of insensitivity is possible through musical language that begs its own way in the environment we would otherwise desire to call worshipful.

Meaning and Significance in Song

Russell Yee draws a distinction between what he terms *shared meaning* and *significance*. His implication is that *meaning* in a worship song is "intended and potentially re-intended by the congregation," and *significance* carries "the import of the meaning to a particular people at a particular time and place. This implies that at least original meaning, once set, remains, but that significance changes. Significance, then, is what is ordinarily meant by, 'What did it mean to you?'"[10] Significance includes the implications, imports, effects, and affects that become attached to a meaning that has been generated throughout the course of time, and

8 Don Saliers and Emily Saliers, *A Song to Sing, a Life to Live* (San Francisco: Jossey-Bass, 2005), 41.

9 Frank Burch Brown, "Christian Music: More than Just Words," *Theology Today* 62 (2005), 224.

10 Russell M. Yee, "Shared Meaning and Significance in Congregational Singing," *The Hymn,* Vol. 48, No. 2, (April 1997), 7.

within the lives of those that encounter that meaning. Church musician scholar Paul Westermeyer posits, "We sing in the idiom of a given time and place even when we may not realize it, indigenizing many things and making them our own."[11] Within the mind and heart of worshipers, music of a specific time and place attaches to the very meaning of that which is being sung. This assignment is very likely at the core of the emotion expressed by church members who are skeptical of stylistic changes in worship music. Attempts at contemporizing older texts from "their day" may actually serve only to make a stylistic chasm wider.

The implications of this dynamic and its application to congregational ministry among itself cannot be overstated. As we will see, the pastoral musician's selection of material will primarily be sensitive to original meaning of text, but a congregation's re-intended meaning, or its composite meaning, and/or its "not meanings;" such as may occur with singing inattentively, singing with resistance to meaning, or singing with preference to emotive or performance effect, can disrupt the ministry we seek to inspire among the participants.

Group Singing

In congregational singing, there is a "groupness" factor. All the previously recognized complexities of music's meaning, significance, and emotion are multiplied yet again when considering the intersubjectivity and intrasubjectivity to others who are part of both perceiving and performing participants. Psychological studies of this process indicate elevated physiological and emotive responses to music through group singing. In experimentation of two groups gathered in the same room, one singing and one not, but the latter hearing the singing of the former, the non-singing group also experienced elevated physiological and mood response, though not as strong as that of the singing group. [12] This groupness also carries potential to strengthen the weaker among us even through the sensed vibration of multiplied voices and through the commonly inhaled and exhaled air upon which our vibrating song rides. In congregational worship song, it seems reasonable that this illustration implies effect and ministry potential among those who are present in worship but not singing, as long as music is exuding from others present who *are* engaged in song.

---

11 Paul Westermeyer, "The Voice of the People: Here, Now, and Beyond," *The Hymn,* Vol. 54, No. 1, (January 2003), 16.

12 Pamela J. Davis, Dianna T. Kenny, and Margaret M. Unwin, "The Effects of Group Singing on Mood," *Psychology of Music,* Vol. 30, No. 2, (2002), 175–185.

While local church autonomy is respected in Baptist life and that as a compilation of individual Christians, all of whom hold personal relationship with Christ as the "called out ones," it still follows that a corporateness is to develop. Yet evangelicals "appear weak when it comes to the corporate awareness that should flow from seeing the church as central in the plan of God."[13] One must question the fierce independent and individualistic nature as serving the anthropocentric tendencies in worship, and not only the fact of selection of individualistic worship material, but also a kind of performance pressure for those who are responsible for making those selections. Their responsibility to other humans, inside or outside the church, both to please and to produce "results" versus responsibility to God and compassion for worshipers, would appear to be in play, again pulling worship toward a human-centeredness.

Music Working Theology

If Frank Burch Brown is correct, and experience certainly seems to confirm such, then "music has its own ways of being religious."[14] Words that have meaning in and of themselves often find a new vitality when set to music. It is well known that a vast majority of history's noted composers at one time or another addressed their craft to biblical and liturgical text. A tendency of genious seems to be to apply its craft to express the mysterious. Is it possible that music can advance theology and worship, and in a sense be a vehicle to "work" them among the people of God? Could music, through its uniqueness as a language that is art that is gift, convey meaning at once with beauty different from other means of expression and communication? Is it possible that music might serve as a language to the heart and from the heart at times when words alone might struggle to inspire, or to speak their own engagement? It seems reasonable that music's elusive quality and nature might carry meaning relative to worship and theology. Calvin Johansson says, "… music is the most logical of all the arts to deal with mystery."[15] Paul Westermeyer points out, "That God, the source and ground of the whole universe, should take flesh among us and care for all of us is irrational, beyond comprehension, alien. The *song* [emphasis mine] will obviously reflect

13 J. I. Packer, *Ancient & Postmodern Christianity*, 125.

14 Frank Burch Brown, "Christian Music: More than Just Words," *Theology Today*, 62 (2005), 224.

15 Calvin Johansson, *Music & Ministry: A Biblical Counterpoint* (Peabody, MA: Hendrickson Publishers, 1984), 91.

this reality."[16] Don Saliers contends that "Human song that arises from a paradoxical world of beauty, injustice, and human suffering is intrinsically theological." He goes on to indicate, "From the very beginning of Christian life and worship, hymns have been a primary carrier of theological import."[17] I would affirm Jeremy Begbie's caution that we not be swept into a *theological aestheticism* where we begin with music "on its own terms," with an open and "value-free" mind, and "then-and-only-then, begin to understand it with a Christian mind." The danger here is that "music itself becomes a new theological master," as if giving us a special access to God.[18] Efforts to enhance awareness of the dynamics of congregational singing must heed the caution that Begbie has noted.[19]

It does seem possible, however, that music might participate in the advancement of certain theological truths. J. S. Bach is perhaps the genius of this interaction. For instance, he employed a descending bass line in *Jesu, der du meine Seele,* which he used repeatedly, depicting the weight of Christ's suffering as he carried the cross, while sopranos join the congregational chorale melody that is uplifting and free.[20] Reggie Kidd recounts his experience of singing *Crucifixus* from Bach's B Minor mass and experiencing the "crushing dissonances" in which the choir experienced "a shared sense of the exquisite horror of what Bach's music portrayed." He reports, "Never have I felt more connected to 'the fellowship of Christ's sufferings.'"[21] Though the necessarily more simplistic nature of congregational music is not normally as musically rich as such works of Bach, nevertheless, the principle and potential remains, and slighter examples can be seen in congregational music.

Disassociating music from text for a moment, I invite you to consider the possibility of music's own way of advancing theological thought. Music may serve to witness to God's goodness in giving us time when it fills the moments with beauty. This may be comparable to the sense of visualizing God's beauty in his creation, such as in a mountain or seaside scene, but music is different in that it is an art that is painted on the canvas of time.

---

16 Paul Westermeyer, "Here, Now, and Beyond," *The Hymn*, Vol. 54, No. 1, (January 2003), 15.

17 Don Saliers, *Music and Theology* (Nashville, TN: 2007), X.

18 Jeremy S. Begbie, *Resounding Truth,* 22.

19 Jeremy S. Begbie, *Theology, Music, and Time* (New York: Cambridge University Press, 2000), 274–279. Begbie distances his discussion of theological advancement through music from a natural theology that is not grounded in divine revelation.

20 Ibid., 124.

21 Reggie Kidd, *With One Voice* (Grand Rapids, MI: Baker Books, 2005), 179.

Time is a necessary ingredient of its conveyance. As Begbie points out, time can be viewed either as a threat or as a gift. The soothing calm of some music that can fill our moments surely depicts the latter. Music is inherently filled with anticipation. Sometimes our expectations are met as anticipated, and at other times, music brings surprise. These surprises can prove satisfactory or not, yet the decision is not ours, but has been determined (we might even say predetermined, separating composing from performing and hearing) for us by the composer. Consider the famous Beethoven's Fifth Symphony theme. The simple eighth note rest at the start of the motif conveys such anticipation. Musical improvisation among a group of musicians only occurs satisfactorily as each player willingly yields to the other. In this way, the playing of music might show forth the interplay of the faith community where each member does not presume the head place at the table (Luke 14:10). Tension and resolution, without which no music is made, may strike mind and heart with the need, fulfillment, and joy of salvation in Christ, the foundation of our relationship to God. Sustained dissonance or ascending passages may build anticipation that displays hope toward eschatological promise.

Western music harmonies are based on the triad in which three separate notes are sounded simultaneously to form one chord. Each note functions differently in relation to the others, but is necessary to the one sound.[22] Can the foundational triad itself be an appropriate symbol for Trinity? Can it even serve as a language that speaks the truth? Can simple harmony both engage and symbolize, and in that sense, "work" the community of faith as *koinonia* in worship? Can the sustained constant of a pedal tone or the recurring beat of a rhythmic pattern convey something of the dependable nature of God? I would contend these attributes are possible. Their effect would seem compounded by being fleshed out through the voice of the congregation in worship.

I hasten to note that the import of music is in no way here being compared to the centrality of Scripture in conveying truth. Rather, I would call focus to the possibilities of sonic order that we call music in all of its simplicity and complexity to aid our worship. We certainly have capacity to overextend its potential, but there seems inherent danger in underestimating its power as well. One problem of our current church culture is to make the great gift of music into little more than a commodity of entertainment.

22 Jeremy Begbie, *Resounding Truth*, 137. Begbie notes that God is not one, and then three, but is one as three from eternity. Though Begbie is connecting this discussion to the music of Bach, I would contend its application to congregational singing is equally valid.

Surely Christian leaders must recognize embedded potential in music for it to aid remembrance, solidify comprehension through repetition thinking on "whatsoever things are good," and impress on human heart and mind in a way that makes concept and truth available for recall.

Studies show that Alzheimer's patients and others with diminutive mental conditions who have practiced singing earlier in life often respond and even sing along in practicing this activity at some level long after other faculties have left them. Such is the case of those having sung hymns in church. Don Saliers points out that this is illustration of the "deeper power of music to encode life, and to make it present—even in the face of cognitive diminishment."[23] Recognizing that music embedded in the believer's mind continues to activate faith constructs in the mind past its capacity to retain other information should surely demonstrate to us the need for its exercise in meaningful ways. Should this not serve as one more reason why the faith community would sing its song with full-orbed participation?

A predominant theological reality of our gathered worship is the interaction of that body itself. As referenced in the previous chapter, this community formation is central to our worship. When the worshiping body sings, the matrix of interactivity is a complex dynamic in and of itself. Harold Best refers to it as "mutual indwelling," which he identifies as a "triple mystery; temples within temple within Temple."[24] All are singing "to" Christ, the Head of the Church, and in a sense, also "with" Christ in Trinitarian worship. Worshipers are singing "to" one another, and "with" one another. Leaders are singing "to" followers, but also "with" followers. Worshipers are singing "to" the world and "on behalf of" the world to God. In congregational singing, the priesthood of the believer is perhaps at its height of function in this matrix of interactive ministry.

I would contend that the question of style of music used in congregational singing is to be addressed in the discussion of worshiping community. Gary Furr and Milburn Price remind us, "Dialogic worship includes and touches the relationships of human participants with one another as well as their relationship to God."[25] Theological deliberation on the text to be sung in gathered worship must be met with questions of appropriateness of music with which it is matched, and that question seems to beg reflection on both

23 Ibid, 6

24 Harold Best, *Unceasing Worship: Biblical Perspectives on Worship and the Arts* (Downers Grove, IL: InterVarsity Press, 2003), 52.

25 Gary Furr and Milburn Price, *The Dialogue of Worship: Creating Space for Revelation and Response* (Macon, GA: Smyth & Helwys, 1998), 51.

its original intention, and on the particular community that is to do the singing in the cultural context of that community.[26] Is this music that can avail this community of *together* worship? Can the community sing this music together in spirit? Reggie Kidd believes "Jesus purges the idolatrous aspects of a culture's music and focuses the yearning for redemption that shows up wherever the *imago Dei* bears the kiss of common grace."[27] Caution is verbalized, however, by people like Daniel Frankforter, who states, "The use of the things of the world in worship may have the effect of rooting us more deeply in the mundane realities from which worship ought to deliver us." Such approach borders on musical legalism, leaving us without music material from which to choose. An "in the world, but not of the world" approach seems to better guide us, especially when tempered by constant surrender to the guidance of the Spirit.

In a narcissistic cultural context, great caution must be exercised because "entertainments center us on ourselves and our pleasures, but Christian worship is meant to indict our egocentrism and lift us out of ourselves to become a people for others."[28] Ongoing attention to community where the assembly seeks to "spur one another on to good works" (Heb 10:24), and "admonish one another with psalms, hymns, and spiritual songs" (Eph 5:19, Col 3:16), while "thinking of one another as better than yourselves" (Phil 2:3) will help leaders select what music is best upon which our words of worship will rise among us. This attention to community follows and is to be included in the highest order and purpose of worship, which is to bring praise and glory to God.

Music and its making can be full of mystery and power. Music making and ministry through it among the worshiping people of God is ripe with potential to assist worship in ways we may not even understand in the moment. Such mystique can further testify to the Gospel of Christ.

Appeal to Pastors

In the opening pages of his book, *Ministry and Music,* Robert Mitchell states, "Every pastor can expect to be involved in church music." He further indicates, "A pastor should be able to relate theology to the goals

26 Another appropriate theological debate questions *absolute beauty,* and whether certain artistic expressions approach the worship of the Creator in a fashion more in keeping with the "best" of our creatorship.

27 Reggie Kidd, *With One Voice,* 127.

28 A. Daniel Frankforter, *Stones for Bread: A Critique of Contemporary Worship* (Louisville, KY: John Knox Press, 2001), 12.

and practices of church music."[29] Music in church has become such a point of controversy for many churches that it may be that many pastors would prefer to ignore such a charge.

Rick Warren began a firestorm in the so-called worship wars when he indicated that church leaders should select music for worship by listening to the radio and discovering what music was the favored style of those in the community.[30] In his more popular book, *Purpose Driven Life,* he further emasculates music's valuation by stating, "Worship has nothing to do with the style or volume or speed of a song. God loves all kinds of music because he invented it all–fast and slow, loud and soft, old and new ... If it is offered to God in spirit and truth, it is an act of worship." Such statements seem dangerously close to implying that God has created sound with neutral valuation, and that ordering and assessing such is completely up to us. In this thinking, music (and by extension, possibly even worship itself) becomes no more than a tool of manipulation. Even if we were to accept that music's value is strictly contextual, it seems our discussion would still continue toward the best of the indigenous music we would then emulate and continue toward questions of knowing and doing that which reflects something of God's character through songs of revelation and that which reflects the best and most humble offering through songs of our response to God. Indeed, the lack of assessment in my view has contributed to the woeful state of musical worship expression in many churches, and has driven many serious musicians from evangelical church environments, lessening the talent pool within the same. Rather than adopting a humanist perspective that says music is in the eye of the beholder, it would seem more in keeping with Christian thought to declare that beauty is in the heart of the Creator.

Adulation of mega church pastors and "success" valuations based upon numbers and budgets of such "bigger than life" settings have driven many pastors and church leaders to accept the anthropocentric approaches of marketing churches. These actions are taken in attempt to grow the numerical base of the church. "Rebranding" and contemporizing the total church environment to appeal to a "target audience" are common actions in the marketing process. Unknowingly, leaders often become so focused on those they seek to reach that they lose sight of worship's foundation in the Gospel of Christ's grace, and shift the message toward a means to be a

29 Robert H. Mitchell, *Ministry and Music* (Philadelphia: Westminster Press, 1978), 11–12.

30 Rick Warren, *Purpose Driven Church* (Grand Rapids, MI: Zondervan, 1995).

better person and get the things out of church that would make life better. Worship, especially its music, is often turned into a weekly theatrical and thematic presentation that far too often appears as an attempt at selling Jesus. The conflicting factors and byproducts of such actions are too numerous to address here, but I would appeal to pastors to read, pray, and counsel long and hard regarding any changes to how the church worships. As with all ecclesial actions, much prayer, scriptural testing, and soul searching should remain central to adjustments in corporate worship design. This is not to say adjustments to worship are not to be made. To the contrary, we are always reforming and refining practice. The caution is toward what the plumb lines are against which adjustments will be measured and assessed. At the point of musical changes, careful counsel with musicians of the church, beginning with the worship music leader, seems crucial to church unity and commonsense leadership protocol.

Appeal to Worship Music Leaders

Regardless of your title, if you are a trained worship music leader, your training and expertise in the area of music must be continuously laid on the altar of humility, service, and worship. Part of your ministry is to offer your best assessments, counsel, and biblical servanthood to your pastor and people. In present-day culture, it is easy to be entrapped by entertainment standards as the goal for musical engagement in church worship. Congregational singing can easily be covered up in musical production and over-production. Quite often, worship leaders wearing in-ear monitors and singing on microphone in front of a well-outfitted band can produce enough decibels in a worship space so as to not have any idea whether the congregation is engaged in spirited worship singing participation or not. Though downplayed by today's church growth culture that reveres stage presence (performance) and popular appeal, there is no substitute for the sacrifice and discipline of academic pursuit in the areas of music and ministry. Over decades, Baptists have been aggressive about developing highly respected learning environments committed to producing church musicians who are well-versed in understanding music as art, skill, developmental tool, and biblically sound means of worship and admonition for local churches. These settings continue to adjust to meet the demands of changing church environments, and I believe still offer the best test of preparation for a person's response to a life calling of ministry through music. That being said, there are numerous practical and accessible aids for selecting and creating music that works for the unique application that is congregational singing in worship (see bibliography). Hymnology studies that include music criteria have been around for many years. Helps for selection of newer worship songs are many and widely varied in approach. Here are a few very basic considerations of music selection for congregational singing:

1. Is the melody singable?
    a. Appropriate ranges and tessitura for singers—plausibly matched with vowels in text (Singing a closed vowel sound on a high pitch can be problematic for today's congregational singer)
    b. Stepwise motion and limited or understandable melodic skips
2. Is the rhythm singable and suited to the lyrics?
    a. Appropriate use of syncopation
3. Does the song "fit" the worshipers who will likely be present?
4. Can the song be understood and serve worship in its intended place in the liturgy progression?
5. Does harmonic structure and accompaniment pattern fit the lyrics and people who will sing the music?
6. Is the song memorable? Some songs are catchy initially, but quite forgettable. Such melodies are likely unworthy to be placed upon the lips of God's people in worship.

Friend and masterful church music practitioner, Mark Edwards, who served for thirty years as Minister of Music for the historic First Baptist Church in Nashville, Tennessee, shares these considerations:

1. Generally speaking, the most usable congregational singing range is C to C; however, notes on either side may be used depending on the tessitura.
2. The best tunes are mostly step-wise melodies
3. The more syncopated or complex the melody/rhythm, the longer it will take a congregation to sing it well and with precision.

4. A lot of people claim that they don't read music, which may be true; however, most can tell when a melody goes up and down.
5. Congregations can be more expressive and more "musical" than we sometimes give them credit for being.
6. Is the accompaniment accessible and does it support the congregation?
7. If the harmony changes frequently, or if the tonal center shifts, a tune will be difficult for congregational singers.
8. Is the tune suitable for congregation or is it better for choir or solo voice? Just because a tune is popular doesn't mean it is suitable for congregational use.

Considerations for quality congregational songs become quite complex and really call for specifications unique to the genre from which an expression emanates. As proliferation of music material intended for use in public worship continues, the worship music leader within congregations must be ever growing in two proficiencies: the ability to become diverse and inclusive, and the ability to be discerning and discriminating.

In the previous chapter, I briefly addressed the ways in which congregational singing addresses the dynamics of worship tensions through the words of congregational singing. While music in general and congregational singing in particular introduce their own tensions, these need not be considered only in their negative connotation, but to the contrary, we find large potential for music's way of presenting and contending with these tensions. Consider the working of Holy Spirit power that engages generations to determine they will serve another generation by joining its music expression in worship as purposeful ministry. Consider the acceptance, no matter at what rate of speed it takes place, of a new song as it comes to be integrated into the worship language of a congregation. Consider the way a song sung for years suddenly finds a new significance given some event in the church family, whether it is joyous or catastrophic. I cannot even say how many times I have personally observed this kind of occurrence. By association of significance, then, the music takes on meaning that carries that remembrance to future gatherings inside and even outside the church. Consider the way a congregation identifies itself, and perhaps outsiders identify it as well, by and through its exuberant expression of worship through singing.

John and Charles Wesley recognized the power of music and singing to aid spiritual renewal and spirited worship. John Wesley, who founded the Methodist Church, wrote "Directions for Singing" in *Select Hymns, 1761,* in which he noted seven of these directions:

> I. Learn these tunes before you learn any others; afterwards learn as many as you please.
>
> II. Sing them exactly as they are printed here, without altering or mending them at all; and if you have learned to sing them otherwise, unlearn it as soon as you can.
>
> III. Sing all. See that you join with the congregation as frequently as you can. Let not a single degree of weakness or weariness hinder you. If it is a cross to you, take it up, and you will find it a blessing.
>
> IV. Sing lustily and with good courage. Beware of singing as if you were half dead, or half asleep; but lift up your voice with strength. Be no more afraid of your voice now, nor more ashamed of its being heard, then when you sung the songs of Satan.
>
> V. Sing modestly. Do not bawl, so as to be heard above or distinct from the rest of the congregation, that you may not destroy the harmony; but strive to unite your voices together, so as to make one clear melodious sound.
>
> VI. Sing in time. Whatever time is sung be sure to keep with it. Do not run before nor stay behind it; but attend close to the leading voices, and move therewith as exactly as you can; and take care not to sing too slow. This drawling way naturally steals on all who are lazy; and it is high time to drive it out from us, and sing all our tunes just as quick as we did at first.
>
> VII. Above all sing spiritually. Have an eye to God in every word you sing. Aim at pleasing him more than yourself, or any other creature. In order to do this attend strictly to the sense of what you sing, and see that your heart is not carried away with the sound, but offered to God continually; so shall your singing be such as the Lord will approve here, and reward you when he cometh in the clouds of heaven.

Though verbiage and sentiment in some of these directions may seem outdated, the value in their spirit remains viable, at the very least, for a glimpse of an ethos present during those days of eighteenth century revival.

I was serving a church as Associate Pastor for Worship. One of our teenagers had been a leader in youth ministry activities, including youth choir. She was the life of the party, a straight A student, and cheerleader at school. A child of divorced parents, she sometimes struggled with emotional unrest. Her Sunday school teacher and I both noticed a significant drop in weight and color missing from her cheeks, and after some joint consultation, agreed to confront her with our concern. After a significant deterioration of her condition, she later began to respond to counseling and support of church, friends, and family. Her departure for college was cause for some anxiety for those of us who wondered how she would handle life on a big campus. The church served as prayer support.

The church had a tradition of welcoming freshman students home at the first Thanksgiving of their collegiate career with a time of special recognition on the Sunday they were home for Thanksgiving break. The congregation was singing, and I had not yet spotted this special young lady for whom I was concerned and for whom the congregation had been praying. The doors at the back of the sanctuary opened and in she walked with two longtime friends. She had recovered to a body size appropriate to her age. Her arms were no longer knotty, and her cheeks were full of the rosy color that had been their pigment before all of this struggle had begun. A powerful message of hope resonated across the congregation in just seeing restoration personified in one of their own. I will not forget the accompanying resonance of the song as we sang, "Give Thanks with a Grateful Heart." I dared to glance at her pew as we sang, "and now let the weak say I am strong, let the poor say I am rich because of what the Lord has done for us." Our eyes connected, tears were running fluently down her rosy cheeks, and I experienced a sudden lump in my throat that I knew would only allow me to rely on the rest of the congregation to proclaim our collective thanksgiving.

The text of that simple chorus was alive among us truly "because of what the Lord had done." It was made so, to some extent, by the contour of the melody that allowed us to soar when we sang "And *now* ..." There was something about the "now" that had to be at the top of that melody line that let us infer the "then" when we had seen a soul slipping. The "now" let us reclaim with joyful gratitude. Call it text painting, or whatever you will. That day it was worship from hearts and voices.

While hymns and worship songs cannot satisfactorily do theology in that they do not satisfy enquired reason or critical examination, they can be integral to the work of theology in practice and application by their function in worship. Brian Wren says, "A hymn invites us, not to step back from faith and examine it, but to step into faith and worship God."[31] Music's power is to be respected and wisely applied.

Worship music leader, take note.

31 Brian Wren, *Praying Twice: The Music and Words of Congregational Song* (Louisville, KY: Westminster John Knox Press, 2000), 351.

Chapter 6

SUNDAY WORSHIP – TIME FOR SINGING

Renewing Commitment To Sunday Worship

Take a Sunday morning drive through any town in America and you will likely come upon a church with cars parked around the building. There may be so many cars that the parking lot will not hold them and adjacent streets must be used for overflow, or there may be only a few cars clustered close to the building's doors. Regardless, most Americans would assume that Christian worship is taking place inside. In fact, Paul Jewett muses, "Were a man from Mars to observe us from his space platform, the most obvious evidence he would have that there are Christians on this planet would be their gathering on the first day of each week at some appointed place and time."[1] He further ponders that if time travel were possible, this first-day Christian assembly could be observed as a weekly repeating pattern that extends throughout history since the first century.

1 Paul K. Jewett, *The Lord's Day: A Theological Guide to the Christian Day of Worship* (Grand Rapids, MI: William B. Eerdmans Publishing, 1971), 12.

In a postmodern, post-denominational, and some would say post-Christian culture, there still remains a notion of, and even value placed upon, the ceremonial gathering for Sunday Christian worship. Certainly, cultural obstacles to Sunday worship gathering subsist worldwide, and the general public remains largely unaware of the true significance of this weekly observance. Declining attendance of Sunday worship has been the trend for Western European churches for decades. In addition, entrepreneurial innovations employed by evangelical church leaders that include worship scheduling choices based on "expansion of your present programming," or simply "providing another option for your people" may misguide both Christians and non-believers to think too pragmatically about Sunday worship. [2] Add to this the confusion over *ecclesiology* and how corporate worship and community fit into Christian faith and practice, and the question of *when* and even *whether* we shall gather for worship may get lost, especially in the free-church tradition.

You may wonder what a focus on Sunday as the day of worship has to do with worship singing. News flash! In order to practice congregational singing in worship, you need a congregation. I could not tell you how many times roundtable conversations with pastors and worship music leaders about the state of church worship has included testimony to poor attendance patterns among church members. Besides being a ridiculously obvious pragmatic ingredient for congregational singing, the congregation's presence in the gathering forms the body that will respond to the self-revealing God. Such gathering finds its impetus in biblical instruction and spiritual unction. It seems to me that it is high time Christians reclaim Sunday as a day of worship. I am not proposing a widespread boycott of businesses that remain open on Sunday, return of the "blue laws" of the 1970s, or a march on city hall after city recreation committees vote to allow the soccer clubs to schedule team play on Sunday. Instead, I am calling upon Christians to be Christian on the day of the week that reminds us that we serve a resurrected Lord, and that we find our identity as a risen people. Call me old fashioned, but I am saying I strongly believe what my parents taught me as a child: that on Sunday, Christians and their families should be in church! A wonderful product (some would say byproduct) of such a restoration movement would surely be a rejuvenated congregational singing. What if, on a

2 Thom S. Rainer and Eric Geiger, *Simple Church: Returning to God's Process for Making Disciples* (Nashville: Broadman & Holman Publishers, 2006), 214.

given Sunday, 80 percent of a congregation's membership was present for gathered worship, rather than the generously reported 40 percent of American evangelical church members who presently attend Sunday church on a regular basis?[3] The excitement of the crowd increase alone would appear to heighten the atmosphere, not to mention dynamics of seeing those who have not attended for some time.

It is my contention that although gatherings for Christian worship can be beneficial *whenever* they might occur, and although attempts to provide gospel witness through Christian worship at a time attractive to non-believers are worthy endeavors, that these cannot substitute for the worship and witness that takes place on the first day of the week, the Lord's Day. I propose that church leaders place a renewed emphasis on gathering for Christian worship on Sunday, the Lord's Day, the day of delight. I want to briefly address the biblical, theological, and historical foundation of Sunday worship gathering, and within my own context, consider how gathered Sunday worship strengthens Baptist identity and provides for spiritual formation. Such renewal of our identity holds good promise to renew vitality in our worship, including our singing. I call your attention to theological and historical underpinnings for Sunday as the day of worship. I would then like to review Baptist practice and consider first day worship in light of that practice and Baptist statements of faith. Finally, I want to invite your thinking as to how a renewed commitment to Sunday as the day of worship might serve renewal in our worship singing.

Theological And Historical Reflection

Human comprehension of any event is dependent upon a dimensional framework of time. Before we can consider the day of worship gathering, we must consider the origin of the time of which we speak. The Genesis account of creation provides the prime differentiation of measured time in the very first creative act of God in His *ex nihilo* creation of light, and its subsequent separation from darkness—the first day. The creation narrative in Genesis 1–2, presented in its seven-part fashion, with six days of creation and a seventh day in which the Creator rests, lays the foundation for all

3 George Barna, *The State of the Church: 2002,* www.barna.org (accessed December 19, 2009).

of life's time pattern and understanding.[4] "Throughout their scriptural narratives, both the Hebrew people and the early Christians underline the sevenfold rhythm built into our innermost beings."[5]

While extra-biblical theories of sevenfold pattern origins exist, evidence is strong that the biblical view maintains its unequivocal credibility. Even those who presume a Babylonian origin adapted by Israel's nomadic ancestors must recognize that "only the ancient Hebrew literature speaks definitely about a seven-day week and a Sabbath."[6] D. A. Carson and collaborative scholars summarize that absent conclusive evidence to the contrary, "we suggest that the Sabbath originated with Israel and that with the Sabbath came the seven-day week."[7]

The Sabbath

The great Saturday/Sunday debate of Christian worship notwithstanding, any discussion of a set day for Christian worship must deal with Sabbath roots. New Covenant people must recognize the Judaic foundation of the Sabbath. "Sabbath rest, as the reenactment of a divine act, provides Jews with a cosmic center."[8] In Exodus we see the Israelites already in the pattern of seventh day observation (Exodus 16:23). The fourth commandment in the Decalogue is recorded in Exodus 20, after which "the law of the Sabbath is found in every stratum of the Jewish

4 While it is not within our scope in this project to present the arguments related to a creation ordinance, such as considered in the major works, Willy Rordorf, *Sunday: The History of the Day of Rest and Worship in the Earliest Centuries of the Christian Church* (Philadelphia: Westminster Press, 1968), 46–51, and Samuele Bacchiocchi, *From Sabbath to Sunday: A Historical Investigation of the Rise of Sunday Observance in Early Christianity* (Rome: The Pontifical Gregorian University Press, 1977), 273–278, and the collective work, D. A. Carson, ed., *From Sabbath to Lord's Day: A Biblical, Historical, and Theological Investigation* (Eugene, OR: Wipf and Stock Publishers, 1982), 346–351, the consideration of such itself draws attention to the assumption of a primordial establishment of pattern and order in time. Notwithstanding some short-lived non-sevenfold patterns, the primary issue in religious practice seems to revolve around the question of which day is to be set aside for particular religious observance; the normative in most of history having been practiced as Saturday for Jews, Friday for Moslems, and Sunday for Christians.

5 Marva J. Dawn, *Keeping the Sabbath Wholly: Ceasing, Resting, Embracing, Feasting* (Grand Rapids, MI: William B. Eerdmans, 1989), 139.

6 Donald A. Carson, ed., *From Sabbath to Lord's Day: a Biblical, Historical, and Theological Investigation,* (Grand Rapids: Zondervan, 1982; Eugene, OR: Wipf and Stock Publishing, 1999), 23.

7 Ibid., 24.

8 Harold Weiss, *A Day of Gladness: The Sabbath among Jews and Christians in Antiquity* (Columbia, SC: University of South Carolina Press, 2003), 1.

Scriptures, a breadth of testimony allotted to no other Old Testament commandment."[9] Recapitulation of the sabbatic theme through the Old Testament expands the notion of Sabbath-keeping into an ethical and social responsibility to be exercised by those chosen to be God's children.

Leviticus 23:3 presents the Sabbath as both a day of rest and a day of assembly. Though God's revelation at times comes through individuals, it comes to and for the collect known as His chosen people. Passages that demonstrate Mosaic conveyance of Sabbath law also reveal a collective nature of these revelations. In Ezekiel 20:11–12 we read, "I gave *them* my Sabbath to be a sign between me and *them*" (italics added). Joseph Pipa says that Isaiah 58:13–14 presents the "purpose" of Sabbath, which has to do with experiencing "the blessings of God that attend it," and manifesting the "solemn promises of great spiritual blessings to *those* who keep the Sabbath day holy." This is to be a "day of delight" that is shared.[10] This collective sense is not constrained to immediacy either, but is to be passed on to future generations—the ongoing people of God, the ongoing assembly.

According to passages like Psalm 92, the day is marked by engagement in such activities as "giving thanks, singing praises, declaring God's loving loyalty and faithfulness, rejoicing with instruments and singing."[11] Such are the perpetual signs of covenant. So, also, are the signs of sanctification, which include sacrifices. D. A. Carson points out the severity of not keeping the Sabbath, namely death. "Though Israel kept the seventh day an official day of rest with the prescribed sacrificial offerings, she also profaned the Sabbath by inward iniquity, greed, idolatry, and rebellion. It is one thing to observe a command, it is another to adhere to the spirit of it. It was those who kept the Sabbath 'with their whole heart' that truly *kept* the Sabbath."[12] This is an important backdrop to Jesus' attitude toward Sabbath, and lays foundation for our approach to a new day set aside for particular keeping.

Jesus and the Sabbath

Luke makes it clear that Jesus went to the synagogue on the Sabbath, "as was his custom," and this in Nazareth, "where he had been brought up" (Luke 4:16). It is significant that Jesus begins to teach with authority in this atmosphere, as these are people who have known him as a carpenter

9 Paul Jewett, *The Lord's Day,* 13.

10 Joseph A. Pipa, *The Lord's Day* (Ross-shire, Great Britain: Christian Focus, 1997), 11–12.

11 D.A. Carson, *From Sabbath to Lord's Day,* 33.

12 Ibid, 32.

boy. His teaching in the synagogue setting on the Sabbath begins to reveal His relationship to that day, first as a faithful participant and eventually revealed as Lord of the Sabbath. The more we learn of Jesus, the more we look back to see foreshadowing, whereby the true spirit of Sabbath would be fulfilled in the Christ.

I recognize the danger of drifting the way of the Pharisees in an overemphasis of religious duty on a religious day. Baptist Thom Rainer places these attitudes in perspective: "The religious leaders had developed a religious system with 613 laws." He goes on to describe the legalistic nature of further divisions, and finally surmises, "Then they spent their days debating whether the divisions were accurate and ranking the commands within each division." We see Jesus, on the other hand, and "... His behavior in the temple gives us amazing insight into the heart of God. Jesus is adamantly opposed to anything that gets in the way of people encountering Him."[13] Marva Dawn describes this conflict as one where Jesus "embraces time instead of space." [14] Succinctly, Jesus embraces the true spirit of Sabbath while others just try to regulate it.

Whether or not you subscribe to the notion of "transference theology," whereby Sabbath (seventh day) sensibilities from the Old Testament are transferred to Resurrection Day (first day) application in the New Testament, you *must* recognize the message contained in points of confrontation that define something of the relationship of Jesus to the Sabbath. The seminal work by Willy Rordorf observes that Jesus' violations of Sabbath were "in their outward appearance inexcusable provocations, but in their inner meaning veiled announcements of his Messianic consciousness."[15] More conservative scholars tend to advocate that Jesus' acts of miraculous proportion toward the needs of people demonstrate His relationship to the Sabbath that is "made for man, not man for the Sabbath" (Mark 2:27). It is not the validity of the Sabbath per se that Jesus confronts, but what kind of activity may be lawfully performed *on* the Sabbath. His message does not argue for the total abrogation of the Sabbath law. The primary point, then, is "The lordship of Jesus over the Sabbath is ultimate; and the insistence on this fact by all four evangelists moves the argument away from purely

---

13 Rainer and Geiger, *Simple Church*, 16–19.

14 Marva Dawn, *Keeping the Sabbath Wholly*, 121.

15 Willy Rordorf, *Sunday: A History of the Day of Rest and Worship in the Earliest Centuries of the Christian Church*, tr. A. A. Graham (Philadelphia: Westminster Press, 1968), 75. It should be noted that Rodorf's conclusion was that Sabbath observation was to be abrogated.

legal questions to essentially Christological ones."[16] For us, "the extended message helps Christians settle internal debates as to permissible Sabbath activities."[17]

From Sabbath to First Day Worship

Paul Bradshaw notes, "The New Testament contains only three texts (Acts 20:7–12; 1 Corinthians 16:2, and Revelation 1:10) which may allude to the Christian observance of Sunday, and even their meaning is a matter of some dispute.[18] Other scholars would say there are more evidences of first-day gatherings. Regardless, there is one thing upon which all agree and that is that the Resurrection took place on the first day of the week (Matt. 28:1ff; Mark 16.2,9; Luke 24:1; John 20:1,19). This event is to take its proper central position in relation to Christian worship gathering, since it is this act that sets Christ and His followers apart for all time. "Only this can really account for the fact that worship on Sunday acquired normative status throughout the Christian world."[19] H. B. Porter points out that it is on the first day that Jesus appears the following week. "It is on the first Day that the Holy Spirit is given." It is "on this day … the aged seer, John is admitted by the Risen Lord to witness the celestial liturgy of the Church of the first-born in the Heavenly Sion." He continues to make the connection noting that the Bible *begins* with the first day which unveils original creative activity of God, and closes with the vision of John on the Lord's Day (Rev. 1:10) of the Christian week. Historically, he notes that "by the end of the first century, the theological basis of Sunday is complete."[20] Through the struggles of the New Testament churches with contentions and factions stemming from Judaizers, Gnostic influences, and the like, still the continued gathering propelled them forward as the gospel was spread first to the Jews and then to the Gentiles, making new disciples, forming new churches, and we believe, observing Sunday worship.

Harold Weiss eloquently sums up the process of transference: "While in the Old Testament the Sabbath came in as a day of rest and in time

16 Carson, ed., *From Sabbath to Lord's Day,* 84.

17 Weiss, *The Day of Gladness,* 95.

18 Paul Bradshaw, *The Search for the Origins of Christian Worship: Sources and Methods for the Study of Early Liturgy* (New York: Oxford University Press, 2002), 178.

19 D.A. Carson, ed. *From Sabbath to Lord's Day,* 240.

20 H. Boone Porter, *The Biblical and Liturgical Meaning of Sunday: The Day of Delight* (Greenwich, CT: Seabury Press, 1960; reprinted Washington, D.C.: Pastoral Press, 1987), 8.

became a day of worship, in the New Testament Sunday came in as a day of worship and became a day of rest."[21] Indeed the "appellation of Sunday in many languages as 'the Lord's day' makes the connection with the resurrection and may also point forward to Christ's return on the 'Day of the Lord.'" The eschatological associations of Sunday are seen also in its patristic designation as the 'eighth day,' going beyond the present week into the future age."[22]

Early Church Fathers, Ancient Church, Reformation, and American Sunday

Justin Martyr describes the Eucharistic liturgy this way:

> We assemble together on Sunday, because it is the first day; on which God transformed darkness and matter, and made the world; and Jesus Christ our Savior rose from the dead on that day; for they crucified him the day before Saturday; and the day after Saturday, which is Sunday, he appeared to his apostles and disciples, and taught them these things which we have presented to you also for your consideration.[23]

From the Didache 14, we observe the instruction, "on the Lord's own day come together and break bread and give thanks, after first confessing your sins, so that your sacrifice may be pure." In these two renderings reflecting the Apostolic Tradition, we can see on the one hand instruction for gathering, and that not only with instruction as to precisely *when* to gather, but also *in what spirit* to gather (Didache); and on the other hand, we can see a glimpse of the liturgy, which itself recapitulates Sunday's place (Martyr). As the church continues to gather, it develops its own culture and indeed, according to Augustine, its own language.[24]

As the church moved toward legalization, it also began to lose its uniqueness. The edict of Constantine in 321 identifying Sunday as a day of rest exemplifies how Christianity, which had experienced such growth, provided an ongoing attraction for political advantage. The continuum of

21 Weiss, *A Day of Gladness*, 4.

22 Geoffrey Wainwright, *The Oxford History of Christian Worship*, ed. Geoffrey Wainwright and Karen B. Westerfield Tucker (New York: Oxford University Press, 2006), 24.

23 Justin Martyr, *First Apology*, 67.

24 Wilken, "Church as Culture," *First Things: A Monthly Journal of Religion & Public Life* (April 2004), 31–36.

church relationship with power and government proved problematic in its diffusion of influence and moral strength. Right away "idle Christians had to be occupied, and the Constantinian church of the Empire became aware of its responsibility to educate the newly Christianized masses.[25] Adaptation of Sabbath-like observance into Sunday practice was an available means of educating. Meanwhile, liturgy was incomprehensible, presented in an unknown tongue amongst great pomp and unintelligible adornment. The environment was ripe for superstition, legalism, and a mysticism that placed the powerful religious keepers in position of perpetual influence and prominence. Sunday-keeping is held in this tension.

In response to exorbitance and abuses of the medieval church, early reformers adopted a "low" theology of the Lord's Day. Luther defended Christian Sunday as a "civil or ecclesiastical institution for the sake of the working classes" who needed more rest. "For Luther the Christian is in no way bound to observe a weekly day of rest or even worship *as a matter of religious obligation.*"[26] Calvin, on the other hand, is more concerned with the "ceremonial" aspect of the fourth commandment of the Decalogue, and indicates its application. The spiritual emphasis is what Karl Barth calls Calvin's "Sabbath mysticism."[27] Despite Calvin's patterns of strict discipline and spiritual gravity, in many locations, Sunday observation continued on a path of libertarianism. In Great Britain, Sunday license evoked the complaint that "in England God was more dishonored and the devil better served on Sunday than on all the days of the week besides."[28] The counterbalance to this libertarian and secularized adaptation of a day free from work, yet often free from worship as well, was the growing influence of Puritanism. While recognizing their aim was to abstain from sin every day of life, Puritans also recognized Sunday as "the day on which we who are Christians rest from our own works, which cannot save us, and mutually strengthen one another in faith, lest any fail to enter into the final Sabbath rest which is laid up for the people of God."[29]

The conflicting environment of Sunday observance in Western Europe and England in particular are important backdrops to American attitudes toward Sunday. Alexis McCrossen puts in perspective the effect of the dynamics. She states, "Declension models—tracing the fall from high to

25 D.A. Carson, ed., *From Sabbath to Lord's Day,* 302.

26 Ibid., *From Sabbath to Lord's Day,* 314.

27 Ibid., 316.

28 Jewett, *The Lord's Day,* 136.

29 Ibid., 151–152.

low or holy to profane—characterize many of the narratives about the history of American culture and society."[30] McCrossen, however, does not present the Sunday "high" to "low" decline as trajectory, but rather as tension whereby the day was a realm where holy day and holiday vied for power.[31] This understanding is important to all subsequent discussions of Sunday in American culture, as it would seem the same tension serves as a canvas even to present day.

Sunday Worship As Baptist Identity And Spiritual Formation

Defining Baptist identity in a discussion of worship presents a complex set of dynamics and an appreciable helping of ambivalence. For one thing, Baptist connections are best described as loose or voluntary. Combine that with a penchant for autonomy and individual freedom and you can see why Bill Leonard says, "Schism, debate, and division are an ever-present reality of Baptist communal relationships." He further states, "In a sense, Baptists created an ecclesiastical and theological framework that ensured controversy, dispute, and division."[32] We mention this divisional tendency because we believe it lends additional credence to those things upon which Baptists *do* agree. One such agreement, by practice and confession, has been weekly Sunday worship gathering as far back as 1609.[33] Contrary practices have only been by small schisms, such as Seventh Day Baptists.[34]

Baptist Confessions

While Leonard reminds us that in Baptist polity "confessions are only guides in interpretation, having no authority over the conscience," still, Baptists often have used confessions of faith as a basis for organizing

30 Alexis McCrossen, *Holy Day, Holiday: The American Sunday* (Ithaca, London: Cornell University Press, 2000), 15.

31 Ibid, 9.

32 Bill J. Leonard, *Baptist Ways: A History,* (Valley Forge, PA: Judson Press, 2003), 7, 9.

33 H. Leon McBeth, *The Baptist Heritage,* (Nashville: Broadman Press, 1987), 91, McBeth includes a partial transcript of a letter from Hughe and Anne Bromhead, which describes a Baptist worship service. This letter from 1609 is the oldest and one of the only recorded descriptions of Baptist worship.

34 H. Leon McBeth, *The Baptist Heritage,* 150, 706–710. While Seventh Day Baptists continue to exist to present day, they have always been small in number by comparison ever since their earliest known congregation, the Mill Yard Seventh Day Baptist Church of London formed around 1653.

congregations, excluding members, dealing with questions of orthodoxy, and ordaining ministers.[35] We look, therefore, to some of these confessions to see their instruction relative to Sunday worship observance. The 1689 London Baptist Confession, the 1833 New Hampshire Baptist Confession, and each of the 1925, 1963, and 2000 renditions of the *Baptist Faith & Message,* a confessional statement of the Southern Baptist Convention, recognize Sunday as a day of worship, private and public. While slight differences exist in each of these confessional statements, the overarching effect is that of essentially a "Christian Sabbath."[36]

Though record of Baptist worship, and certainly of Baptist liturgy, is scant at best, we would still strongly contend that Sunday worship gathering and observance of Sunday as the Lord's Day are central aspects of Baptist identity. A review of Baptist history publication indexes is likely to associate "Sunday" with "Sunday school," as its foremost organizing program, or the "Baptist Sunday School Board" (now Lifeway Christian Resources), the name of the Southern Baptist Convention's publishing arm until its name change in 1998, or even the fiery early twentieth century evangelist, Billy *Sunday.* Indexes reflect the use of Sunday as a recognized moniker, but much less a revered holy day, even though actual practice would indicate a different ethos. I would contend that one reason for the lack of emphasis in recorded history is a presumption of weekly Sunday worship as a fact of Baptist life.[37] We could easily assume that other evangelical groups have realized similar experience.

Spiritual Formation

Augustine recognized that Christian culture has its language, and *that* language is at once forming the culture. Sunday recitation is irreplaceable as words and phrases like, "obedience, grace, long-suffering, image of God, suffering servant, adoption, will of God—when used again and again—form our imagination and channel our affections." Recitations of psalms, said or sung in our worship, translate words of the psalmist into words that

35 Bill Leonard, *Baptist Ways,* 7.

36 The 1689, and 1833 Confessions actually refer to Sunday as the "Christian Sabbath." The 1925, and 1963 renditions of the *Baptist Faith & Message* adopted by Southern Baptist Conventions refer to Sunday as the first day, the Lord's Day, and call for public and private worship, and abstinence from certain amusements. The 2000 rendition seems to relax the abstinence requirement in a manner that could be read as somewhat libertarian.

37 McBeth, *The Baptist Heritage: Four Centuries of Baptist Witness,* 739–780. The index here serves as an example.

we use to praise.[38] Reminding worshipers of beloved departed who have sung our songs and spoken our words helps to form our lives together for coming days of uncertainty with confidence in eternal God.

To affirm faith identity, people "need to be reminded of the larger religious vision of which they are a part and the heritage from which they have come."[39] Congregational gathering for worship is central to spiritual formation for individual persons in Christ, and for the Lord's church in the local setting. Marva Dawn says it "schools the followers of Christ in God's metanarrative."[40] It would seem significant that the timing of such a gathering would "work" that formation by virtue of the day chosen for gathering. "Worship is the prime identity-creating practice of the Church. It is the constituting activity, repeated habitually for the sake of clarity, which discloses God in Christ as the source, character, meaning, and end of the Church."[41]

Conclusions

Biblical and historical review lead us to theological positions and conclusions that become the basis of our faith and form our practice. While some issues have remained, and apparently shall remain in tension until Jesus returns, there are foundational stack poles upon which practice may be exercised with spiritual confidence and we believe appropriate orthopraxy. As we consider the subject at hand, the first theological position we profess is that God, as author of all of creation, is the giver of time *(chronos)* and places life as we know it within that dimension. His redemption of humans occurs in time which He uniquely enters and acts *(kairos)* in Jesus Christ, the Redeemer, Savior, and is ever present in the Holy Spirit. God is fully deserving of gratuitous and worshipful living for who He is, and particularly in response to His provision through Jesus' sacrifice and resurrection. Secondly, we would agree that through the report of God's original pattern and through the command of the Decalogue, with resultant promise of consequence that the Lord intends

38 Wilken, "Church as Culture," 35.

39 William McCready, "The Role of Sunday in American Society: Has It Changed?" in *Sunday Morning: A Time for Worship*, ed. Mark Searle (Collegeville, MN: The Liturgical Press, 1982), 115.

40 Marva J. Dawn and Eugene Peterson, *The Unnecessary Pastor: Rediscovering the Call* (Grand Rapids, MI: William B. Eerdmans, 2000), 217.

41 Rob Hewell, "The Politics of *Leitourgia:* Transcending Nationalism in Evangelical Worship in the United States (D. Min. diss. San Francisco Theological Seminary, 2006), 147.

some particular worship observation of a day that we believe includes a collective or gathered assembly emphasis. Thirdly, we believe that Christian worship as a means of edification, communion, and witness of the body of Christ is best observed on Sunday, providing reminder that this is the first day, the day of Resurrection, the day of gathering, and the Lord's Day which reminds us to anticipate the coming *parousia*. We believe that our Baptist ecclesiology is in much need of strengthening at these points, but it is these points as well that offer opportunity for just such strengthening to occur.

Historical evidence of gathered Sunday worship strengthens our resolve that what we observe in the New Testament among believers in glimpses of first-day gathering for worship is an intended pattern that has been affirmed by repeated practice among believers. Though vulnerable to tainting by political, institutional, and anthropocentric influences throughout history, we believe the spirit of genuine Sunday worship has appropriately developed into a kind of Christian Sabbath. In that sense, the day some say is a recurring "little Easter" has been repeatedly resurrected and subject to *semper reformanda*. This has resulted in what Dorothy Bass describes as joyful worship, which "restores us to communion with the risen Christ and our fellow members of his body, the church," which she notes is essential to Christian Sabbath.[42] The assembling itself signifies the body coming to fellowship and following the admonition of Hebrews to "forsake not the assembling of yourselves" (Hebrews 4:24).

In a post-denominational Christian environment, Southern Baptists continue to seek an understanding of their own identity that embraces theological distinctives, yet places their practice within the larger context of all or most evangelicals. It is at this point that we believe great restraint must be exercised among Baptist pastors and leaders when reflecting upon popular evangelical writing that either glorifies numerical "success" based upon entrepreneurial pragmatism that sometimes supersedes biblical, historical orthopraxy, or that ignores gathering altogether in sight of a presumed postmodern Christian spiritualism that includes only loose, often uncommitted connection to a local church body. Sunday worship, and even gathering itself, must not be ignored as unneeded traditionalism. Dissing the local church as "a crutch or excuse for wimpy faith" seems to serve more to embolden the undisciplined believer who is uninterested in submitting to any ecclesial authority or connecting "spiritual" with whole

42 Dorothy C. Bass, *Receiving the Day: Christian Practices for Opening the Gift of Time*, (San Francisco: Jossey-Bass, 2000), 70.

life and world reconciliation than it does to encourage a Christian faith "revolution."[43] More constructive, perhaps, would be renewed efforts at local church worship that is authenticated by central understandings of its dynamics including the gathering act itself. For Baptists, we believe this could prove a kind of discovery of something that has been available all along; the charisma of Sunday as its own dynamic of worship in its ever-present meaning, the Resurrection and coming Day of our Lord. Such a rejuvenation would seem to aid the restoration of recognizing the importance of the Lord's Day for mature believers who form the church body and would also serve to develop a sense of excited anticipation in the hearts and minds of children and teenagers who would be exposed to this renewal and would learn by practice the joy that lives counterculturally to the narcissism of the secular world.

In consideration of congregational singing's need for, first of all, a congregation, and at that, a congregation that will sing, I believe there is need and rich potential in the renewal of Sunday worship. Revering the day sets a tone for the weekend that finds its exclamation point to be a gathering of the church for celebration, admonition, and reflection in worship. Worship singing is heightened when a spirit of expectation prevails. Sunday worship holds great potential as its first-day understanding would presume. Encouragement and admonition among believers reflects the worship of the New Testament, and holds in proper perspective the understanding of all of life as worship. This is not just a matter of getting spiritually jazzed for a new week. Renewal at the beginning of the week provides reminder of the Lordship of Christ in His overcoming power that handles death and the grave. Singing our worship in a mode of receiving God's grace-gifts on the Lord's Day helps remind us of His resurrected life in us come Monday and Tuesday and the rest of the week.

43 George Barna, *Revolution: Finding Vibrant Faith Beyond the Walls of the Sanctuary* (Carol Stream, IL: Tyndale House Publishers, 2005), 104ff. Barna's provocative work is well-presented, yet his prediction seems to abdicate the work of a local church expression replacing it with "church" connection that has no structure per se, seemingly only a kind of missional function.

Chapter 7

SACRED ACTS – SACRED SINGING

"What is going on here?" Perhaps no question is more potent or in some ways as unanswerable in regard to the regular weekly worship of our churches. William Willimon poses this question and says of the diagnosis of worship, "If we, as pastors, could learn to diagnose and analyze people's worship, here would be a rich resource of insight and revelation."[1] Of course, such knowing is neither really possible, nor is it actually desirable. Worship is between God and His people. Individually and corporately, most evangelicals understand at some level the Lord's instruction, "these words are to be in your heart" (Deut 6:6). The engagement that takes place in worship is spiritual, and final evaluation belongs to God Himself. David Dockery reminds us that in order for worship to be renewed, "we need to emphasize that worship is primarily spiritual and symbolic. Worship is only possible in and by the Holy Spirit, who prompts our love and praise of God. At the same time, we need to rediscover the resources available to help us highlight those symbols handed down to us by Christ, the apostles, and the experiences of

1 William H. Willimon, *Worship as Pastoral Care* (Nashville: Abingdon Press, 1979), 64.

the saints of the ages."[2] In this chapter, I want to invite your consideration of how congregational singing can help us do the highlighting. Webster defines "sacred" as that which is "set apart, or consecrated for the service or worship of a deity." I ask that you consider the sacred nature of worship itself, and thus consider aspects of weekly worship for their sacred nature. As we consider sacred activity in worship, I ask you to reflect on ways that singing has assisted your own faith journey in understanding the nature and import of these sacred acts. We will review these actions in the order of fourfold worship process, which I believe is a usable liturgy order for evangelical worship just as it is for more formal environments of Christian worship. Then we will consider the ordinances, and other worship acts and the opportunity each present for ministry through sacred song and singing.

Gathering

The worship assembly is an expression of what it means to be *ekklesia,* the church, the "called out ones." While we leaders might want to know "what is going on here" by looking into the mind of each gathered worshiper present in the assembly, it is more intrinsic to our responsibility as leaders to help the worshipers understand that the gathering is itself an act of worship and that the gathered body is testimony to Christ Himself. In worship we lift up Christ! Gathering for worship is less about events in the lives of the people of the church and more about the event of worship itself as it remembers the events of God, and expresses the ongoing reality of God at work in the world.

"The connection between worship and spirituality are made in God's story."[3] In our narcissistic culture, we forget far too often that authentic Christian worship centers in God's story, not our own. Robert Webber reminds us over and again that the miracle is not that God joins our story, but rather that He lifts us into His story. It is important that our entrance into corporate worship be characterized by expectancy, gratitude, and humility. Our entrance to worship comes only because of the miraculous provision that God has made that we might gather with Him; that we might actually "come into His presence with singing" (Ps 95). Surely our entrance into worship, the gathering itself, should be a sacred act of spiritual and symbolic worship. Isaiah 6:1–8

2 David Dockery, *Southern Baptist Consensus and Renewal* (Nashville: B&H, 2009), 125.

3 Robert Webber, *Ancient-Future Worship: Proclaiming and Enacting God's Narrative* (Grand Rapids, MI: Baker Books, 2008), 24.

is a passage oft-referenced for its valuable outline of a worship encounter with God. The passage begins with Isaiah's entrance into the Temple, which leads to his vision of the Lord, "high and lifted up." In the New Testament we are told of a "new and living way" (Heb 10: 20) to enter with confidence into the Holy Place. In the psalms we read Psalms of Ascent that give a picture of anticipation and joyous gathering.

Robert Webber brought renewed emphasis on gathering for corporate worship. In his fourfold worship pattern, he recognizes the first "fold" as "characterized by the simplicity of entering into God's presence."[4] Stanley Hauers recognizes the movement itself, stating, "Gathering indicates that Christians are called from the world, from their homes, from their families, to be constituted into a community capable of praising God (Matt. 28:16–20)."[5]

Congregational singing is one of the most effective means of marking the gathering of worship. Singing provides a means for the body to call itself into confession and spirited praise. Priesthood of the believer is practiced as members call on one another to recall their identity in Christ through Whom we bring the sacrifice of praise (Heb 13:15–17). The declaration of corporate praise, whether through a majestic traditional hymn or a joyous contemporary chorus patterned after a psalm, serves as a symbolic reminder that though we are many, we become one in Christ. Singing together provides us a means of laying down our preferences in order to humble ourselves that Jesus Christ may be praised. Drawn and enlivened by the Holy Spirit's presence, the gathering can actually serve as both revelation of God through the recounting of His blessings and worthiness, and response to God through our common gratitude and praise.

Too often, we as believers take for granted the gathering together with the body of Christ. This wrong attitude is one of the primary reasons worship attendance is inconsistent in our churches. A genuine change in such an attitude would surely benefit us and make our singing more joyous as we welcome one another through acts of hospitality, welcome, and community praise. There is potential for renewed spiritual fervor in remembering the specialness of Sunday as the day of our Lord's resurrection. We can enter His gates with thanksgiving and His courts with praise. We can come to gather, worshiping!

---

4 Robert E. Webber, *Planning Blended Worship: The Creative Mixture of Old and New* (Nashville: Abingdon Press, 1998), 51.

5 Stanley Hauers, "The Liturgical Shape of the Christian Life: Teaching Christian Ethics as Worship" in *Essentials of Christian Community,* David F. Ford and Dennis L. Stamps, eds. (Edinburgh, Scotland: T&T Clark Ltd., 1996), 40–41.

Word

As has already been stated, the two consistent activities through all of Baptist worship are (and have been) preaching and singing. For many, the sum total of what it means for us to be "people of the book" revolves around the hearing of the preached Word of God. Certainly, preaching is central to evangelical worship by time allotment and by focus within evangelical liturgy. A certain amount of symbol can be attributed to this centralization itself. In chapter eight, we will join other voices in calling for a deeper saturation of Word through the whole of worship, but suffice it to say at this point, worship renewal can be served by singing that assists our reverence for the Holy Scriptures. Most pastoral musicians select music that directs focus toward the theme of the sermon when they have such information in sufficient time to make those arrangements. Over time, most leaders will have opportunity to work with preaching pastors who will preach expositional messages and will give them the Scripture passage and focus in time to help the congregation prepare to hear through the singing of songs related to the central theme of the message.

Throughout my own ministry, I have had privilege to work with some pastors who placed a premium on sermon planning for months at a time, and I have also served with other preachers who struggled to prepare from one Sunday to the next, and ended up with "Saturday night specials," in which final decisions were being made for Sunday's sermon the night before. Those who know something of this dilemma may resonate with the old story about the pastor and music director who prepared separately. The pastor preached a scathing temperance message in which he called for all alcohol from the county to be gathered up and hauled to the local tributary and thrown in the river. The red-faced musician then stood to lead the selected hymn of response, "Shall We Gather at the River." I have never had anything quite that comical occur, but I have listened to sermons and had visions of singing dance in my head that could have helped prepare the people to hear the Word by singing the Word, had I only known what the message Scripture and theme were in time to select songs accordingly.

Regardless of sermon theme, one surefire means of aiding Word-centered worship through congregational singing is to focus worship singing on the Word itself. One of my professors, Dr. Connie Cherry, reminded those of us who plan worship that "the Word of God is more powerful than anything else anyone can say or sing in worship."[6] Given appropriate attention, singing the Word surely draws attention to the Word and helps to prepare worshipers for God's revelation through the spoken Word. Worship music leaders should consider singing songs that call specific attention to the Word itself or that directly prepare us to listen, hear, and open our hearts and minds. A splendid example of such a song from new hymn literature is the Keith Getty and Stuart Townend song, "Speak, O Lord."

Speak, O Lord, as we come to You
To receive the food of Your Holy Word
Take Your truth plant it deep in us
Shape and fashion us in Your likeness,
That the light of Christ might be seen today
In our acts of love and our deeds of faith
Speak, O Lord and fulfill in us
All Your purposes for Your glory.
Teach us, Lord, full obedience,
Holy reverence, true humility;
Test our thoughts and our attitudes
In the radiance of Your purity.
Cause our faith to rise; cause our eyes to see
Your majestic love and authority.
Words of power that can never fail
Let their truth prevail over unbelief.

Speak, O Lord, and renew our minds;
Help us grasp the heights of Your plans for us
Truths unchanged from the dawn of time
That will echo down through eternity.
And by grace we'll stand on Your promises,
And by faith we'll walk as You walk with us.
Speak, O Lord, till Your church is built
And the earth is filled with your glory. [7]

---

6 Constance Cherry, from class lecture notes in the class "Music and the Arts in Worship" at the Robert E Webber Institute for Worship Studies, June, 2006.

7 Keith Getty & Stuart Townend, "Speak, O Lord" in *Baptist Hymnal 2008,* Thank You Music, 2006.

In a later chapter, we will consider ways to utilize this song in a concerted effort toward renewal, but for the moment I encourage you to simply review the text and to note its reverential attitude toward the Word of God and the respect for its power. The song continually draws its focus back to God's work. To begin with, the song is expressed *to* God in worship; it is a prayer. The song repeatedly asks for the Lord's work *through* the Word: "Take Your truth plant it deep in us …" "Test our thoughts and our attitudes …" and does not ask for this work to benefit us as an end in itself, but rather reroutes the purpose to the appropriate result of worship, the Lord's glory: "… fulfill in us all Your purposes for Your glory," "… till Your church is built and the earth is filled with Your glory."

Songs of Word-focus can assist worshipers as they sing their preparation to hear from the Holy One. Whether we sing traditional hymns, such as "Holy Bible, Book Divine," "Word of God Across the Ages," or "Wonderful Words of Life," or we sing more recent compositions like "Ancient Words," "Thy Word," or "Word of God, Speak," the moment of preparation to hear from God's Word is pregnant with spiritual potency for individual worshipers and for the collective gathered body. Singing words of worship may help worshipers prepare to receive God's spoken Word as a sacred act of worship.

Table

The Table of the Lord, called Communion, Eucharist, or the Lord's Supper, has been a distinguishing component of worship expression for all Christian denominations through history. As the son of a Baptist preacher who has been a part of Baptist piety and worship ethos my whole life, I have benefited greatly from my experiences of recent years through study and relationships with Christian brothers and sisters of other faith traditions. I have been particularly interested to share deep conversation with those whose traditions lead them to a more sacramental view of the Table than my own faith tradition. This interaction has caused me to research the theological strains within my own denomination more fully, as well as studying to gain a better grasp on what separates my tradition from others and what holds potential to unite us with other communions.

I am neither qualified, nor is their space or focus here for an essay on theological sensibilities to sacramental or memorial understandings of the Lord's Supper observance. Rather, what I would like to briefly address is its import and treatment in Baptist worship environments.

I concur with others that, very often, evangelical worship reflects many inadequacies brought about through an Enlightenment mindset that "desupernaturalizes" the world by basing worship gatherings in rationalization tendencies and maintaining that worship must be first and foremost a human experience (anthropocentric). I trust that readers of other faith traditions will forgive the diatribe and will be able to see in this section the potential for congregational singing to support the ethos of communion worship regardless of the particular piety. Though far too infrequently practiced in some denominations, including my own, the Table is undeniably central to Christian worship, as demonstrated and taught in the New Testament and through patristic practice. Robert Webber and others have suggested that faith traditions that do not offer weekly Lord's Supper observance represent Eucharistic elements through other practices: the altar call, prayers of thanksgiving, offerings, preaching, confessional prayers, assurance of pardon, Gospel proclamation through song and Word, acts of hospitality, and recitation of covenants.

It seems to me that worship planners in free-church tradition must give ongoing consideration to the spirituality of the worship environment and liturgy of worship, and include Eucharistic elements in weekly Sunday worship. On Sundays when the Lord's Supper is not being observed, perhaps additional consideration would best be given to ways worshipers can be reminded of the work of God in Christ (remembrance), the gratitude that must be our response to His salvific acts (thanksgiving), and the work of the Holy Spirit moving among us as we greet one another, hear His Word, and become unified in the mission He has given us (real presence). We will discuss Sundays of Lord's Supper observance as ordinance toward the end of this chapter and revisit the topic in the chapter admonishing renewal.

Through all the dynamics mentioned in previous chapters, congregational singing assists worshipers in their gatherings to become aware that Christ has been faithful to His Word of Gospel that "where two or three come together in my name, there am I with them" (Matt 18:20), and thus is present and at work. Recognizing the context of that verse to be one of reconciling differences, surely it is the presence of Jesus among us through the Holy Spirit that brings about healing of relationships. Singing God's story of creation, incarnation, atonement, resurrection, and ascension will surely assist us in remembrance (*anamnesis*). Singing our mission, Holy Spirit power, and the promised return of *Christus Victor* will surely assist our worldview toward eternal purpose and shared ultimate victory (*prolepsis*). In the absence of weekly Table observance, perhaps such singing can move our worship ethos toward a eucharistic spirituality in the times between the observations of the ordinance.

Sending

There is much talk today about "missional church." It seems to me that if we are following Jesus Christ there is no other kind (of church). By popular understanding and by definition, evangelicals are known as people on a mission. A centerpiece of most churches that would give themselves an evangelical designation is a commitment to be on a mission to share Christ with others in word and deed. The Great Commandment offers irrefutable instruction from the lips of Jesus Himself to "go and make disciples ..." (Matt 28:19–20). The command is one of the most repeated themes of preaching and teaching in evangelical churches, beginning with Baptists who boast the largest vocational missionary force in the world and who have practiced a repeated emphasis on personal evangelism as an aspect of Christian living. Certainly the Great Commission is to be a part of the fabric of a church's organizational structure and process, but leaders would do well to recall its orientation in Christian worship. If worship is indeed an offering of our whole life (Rom 12:1), then we leave the gathered worship community as those who are sent to worship as we "go into all the world."

Many churches have a "closing song" that may serve to end the Sunday morning worship hour. While such a song often derives its meaning as a benediction or blessing to end what has been taking place in the corporate meeting, worshipers may need to better understand the prayer (said or sung) as a segue from worship in the gathered place to worship in daily living. Worship in going is a needed emphasis for most of us in contemporary culture. Since music has a way of hanging in our brain after the sonic event has ended, perhaps we need to be intentional about singing to accompany our sacred act of sending.

The Ordinances

Baptism and Lord's Supper are the ordinances or sacraments in which most evangelicals participate as sacred acts of worship. Baptists and other evangelicals have tended to shy away from the term "sacrament" as a pushback from Roman Catholic understandings of transubstantiation, and/or to differentiate from other Protestants who perceive Baptism and

Eucharist as means of divine grace. As mentioned previously, divisions regarding these understandings are widely varied, not even uniform within individual denominations themselves, and somewhat confusing in differentiating between "real presence" versus "sign and symbol" as language fails to serve the complete expression of spirituality and mystery of faith as it pertains to these worship acts.

Whatever we might feel about God's presence in the water of baptism in worship, we can agree that His Holy Spirit imparts the full message of gospel through the baptism moment. Whatever the particular vehicle may be, it would seem the Spirit is free to act in accordance with God's design. Stanley Grenz states it well: "The goal toward which baptism points and which it anticipates is already being accomplished by the renewing work of the indwelling Holy Spirit, whose presence is the pledge of the eschatological fullness of salvation (2 Cor 1:22; 5:5; Eph 1:14) and whose reception is likewise symbolically experienced in baptism."[8] If baptism of the Holy Spirit has already come to the individual being baptized, then logically, the Spirit is present as the individual enters the water and is also in the room filled with others who have previously experienced the same.

Formal statements regarding the meaning and practice of baptism in Southern Baptist confessionals are simple and straightforward, but give no indication of its placement within a worship environment. Baptist tradition and official statements indicate that practicing the *ordinance* as a performative act of worship for the candidate and participating church body in the corporate worship setting conveys the testimony of the new believer, serves as the "prerequisite for church membership," and witnesses to the gospel message.[9] Even when the emphasis of baptism is a non-*sacramental* approach, the enactment is not restricted to a rationalistic cognitive process, but can engage worshipers in the great mystery of salvation and redemption itself. This fits with what C. S. Lewis describes as transposition. He states, "With whatever sense of unworthiness, with whatever sense of audacity, we must affirm that we know a little of the higher system which is being transposed."[10]

8 Stanley Grenz, "Baptism and the Lord's Supper as Community Acts" in *Baptist Sacramentalism*, 93.

9 *The Baptist Faith & Message, 2000*, provides a short paragraph declaring the meaning and mode of baptism. The statement makes it clear that the ordinance is a symbol of the new believer's testimony, and that because it is a church ordinance it is prerequisite to church membership and related privileges. *The Baptist Faith & Message, 2000,* available at http://www.sbc.net/bfm/bfm2000.asp; Internet.

10 C. S. Lewis, *The Weight of Glory* (San Francisco: Harper San Francisco, 2001), 105.

I contend that a deepened understanding of baptism, a heightened awareness of God's presence in worship during the act of baptism, and an application of congregational singing to assist in the engagement of the congregation in communal worship during baptism can serve the purpose of worship renewal.

Touching and hearing water, considering its death power and the faith to plunge oneself under its influence, could be profound connections for worshipers. Consideration of water—such as in the Spirit hovering over the water before the world began (Gen1:2), the deliverance acts through the flood (Gen 6–9), through the Israelites escape from Egypt (Ex15) and (1 Cor 10:1–2), our birth through water, and by the same means, the birth and thus Incarnation of our Lord, Jesus' own baptism in water by John (Jn 1), Jesus' first miracle turning water into wine (Jn 2), Jesus' reference to His provision of *living water* (Jn 4), the gushing of water mixed with blood from Jesus' side at the cross (Jn 19:31–37), the gathering of all the Saints at the Crystal Sea (Rev 22), and even the notion of thirst as the most basic of human needs—all seem to hold rich opportunity for enhancing worship at the pool of water.[11]

Rite and Renewal

A worship dictionary defines *rite* as "a formal act constituting a religious observance." These "formal acts" connect with natural ones; for instance, the Lord's Supper with eating, baptism with bathing. The dictionary states that "rites are not artificial constructions but rest in the natural order and in the sphere of human activities, and unless this connection is preserved they can easily degenerate into magic or intellectualism."[12] So, a logical concern is how we preserve the connection.

In the past, Baptists have tended to reject the idea of r*ites* and/or *rituals* identified as such because of the same aforementioned anti-Roman Catholic sentiments, and more recently perhaps by reason of a presumption that *rites* have little spiritual, pragmatic, or entertainment value. Leaders protect their opportunity to improvise ambiance and order of worship by avoiding ritual terminology, by obscure placement of service items (baptism and Lord's Supper are often placed at the very beginning or end of a worship

11 Reggie M. Kidd, "Baptism's Story," (class notes and visual presentation to DWS 704 at the Institute for Worship Studies, 12 June, 2007).

12 J. G. Davies, editor *The New Westminster Dictionary of Liturgy and Worship* (Philadelphia: Westminster Press, 1986), 468.

service as if tacked on to worship), or by other dismissive means. Some continue to expound against the issues of ritualism. This position is not without merit, of course, as has been cautioned by many Christian leaders lest we be led "to an emphasis on outward manifestations of piety and worship, to the neglect of the appropriate inward attitude of faith," as seen in Jesus' controversy with the Pharisees. "Yet Jesus did not abolish ritual lustrations, despite his strong condemnation of their misuse." [13]

We live (and worship) in the tension between the need to be consciously and willfully engaged with the holy and the need to accept that which is holy as "other," understanding that "reality is larger than me." "The usefulness of a ritual is that it takes a human action that is understood as essential to our ordinary lives and removes it from our immediate 'say-so,' protects it from our tinkering and revisions and editing, sets it apart from our moods and dispositions."[14] Protecting the action (baptism) and its placement encourages our attendance to it as something separate from ourselves that draws *us* into *its* reality. The uncomfortable truth is that such "otherness," even "numinous," must remain outside our ability to over-engineer it in worship in order to maintain its influence. And this is the very thing to which we worship leaders are tempted to attend. Eugene Peterson reminds us that "we cannot be too careful about the words we use; we start out using them and then they end up using us."[15] Leaders serve the people well by preparing the baptismal candidate and church through informed pastoral care prior to the baptism in worship, and then by allowing the biblical words and dynamic of God's presence in the worship and through the *rite* itself to serve in this transitional *rite of passage.*[16]

I contend that worship leadership in Baptist contexts would do well to allow baptism a focal place in public gathered worship as a "rite of commitment," an "ordained occasion when one confesses that she or he has made a faith commitment to Christ. When faithfully and rightly observed, baptism may also be a means of grace, not in the sense that it saves, but in the sense that it is the occasion where God acts to seal and confirm the blessings and promises of the gospel."[17] I contend that the

13 Manley Beasley-Murray, *Baptism in the New Testament,* 10.

14 Eugene Peterson, *Christ Plays in Ten Thousand Places,* 205.

15 Ibid., 38–39.

16 M. Mahan Siler, "Rites of Passage: A Meeting of Worship and Pastoral Care" in *Review and Expositor,* 85 (1988), 51–61.

17 Hammett, *Biblical Foundations for Baptist Churches,* 276–277.

ritual enacted as worship will draw worshipers into its reality and confront the public with the gospel message. Yes, it is symbol, but what richness surrounds this sign.

If rite and ritual are to serve worship renewal, perhaps evangelicals need to temper the fear of the magical, mystical presentation and learn something of the fervor in the orthodox understanding of the rite's power. "The proper celebration of Baptism is indeed the source and the starting point of all liturgical renewal and revival. It is here that the Church reveals her own nature to herself, constantly renews herself as a community of the baptized." For the Orthodox, it is an essential function of baptism to "always *renew* the Church."[18]

In baptism, we hear the declaration of Trinity, baptizing "in the Name of the Father, the Son, and the Holy Ghost," in one of the few occasions for performative utterance in Baptist life. In baptism, we observe the gospel presentation almost completely without words. In baptism, we find opportunity for the gathered congregation to make some one-time verbal response to affirm and welcome the new sister or brother being immersed. Whether this is an "Amen," or the contemporary applause, the ritual engagement with the whole body to the new part of the body holds powerful significance. In baptism, we worship in the picture not only of individual and collected individual faiths, but we affirm the entirety of salvation history and declare the full gospel truth. It would seem that this is fertile soil for the work of the Holy Spirit, Who is fresh upon the new believer, and refreshed in the life of His church having been both expanded and reminded of His presence and power to save and renew. Timothy George connects baptism and the Lord's Supper with declaration of the Word in that "they are 'the visible words of God' proclaiming in visual, tactile and olfactory ways what the preacher has declared audibly in the exposition of holy scripture."[19]

Congregational singing in worship serves many purposes. It conveys and shapes theology, builds community, and allows participation in mystery in a manner unique to its properties in human experience. Congregational singing is well-suited to serve through all of its characteristics during worship through baptism.

---

18 Alexander Schmemann, *Of Water & The Spirit: A Liturgical Study of Baptism* (Crestwood, NY: St. Vladimir's Seminary Press, 1974), 38.

19 Timothy George, "The Sacramentality of the Church" in *Baptist Sacramentalism,* eds. Anthony Cross and Philip Thompson (Eugene, OR: Wipf and Stock Publishers, 2003), 28.

Christian leaders have recognized for a long time that "music shapes and conveys theology, and is a point of engagement with broader culture."[20] Aristotle was convinced that the character of music had an influence on the character of people. Clement of Alexandria championed music that promoted 'composed manners.' Augustine recognized the mysterious relationship between certain modes in song and various human emotions—and so on, through the medieval philosophers, the Reformers, and well beyond."[21] John Bell points out, "What we sing shapes the way we understand and think of God." Furthermore, "what we sing shapes what we believe."[22] Don Hustad sees how the activity works both sides of the worship dialogue when he states, "congregational singing is both revelation of God and response to God, since great hymns always have been saturated with scripture and thus become expressions of biblical theology."[23]

In the case of baptism, congregational song provides opportunity for theological engagement (proclamation and ingestion) with specific baptism texts or biblical reference to subjects that are a part of baptism, like water, washing, cleansing, new life, the Holy Spirit, and the church. This direct engagement is the most obvious benefit of congregational singing's import to worship during baptism, and this not just through the cognition of the text and tune as emotive information. In congregational singing, the singing itself has its effect on worship. For the individual, "the whole person may be involved: the body, the mind, the emotional self, and the will." In addition, "human experience finds 'aesthetic transcendence' in both poetry and music."[24] Thus the involvement is with the whole being and engages self at a level unique to the experience. This engagement can assist the worshiper to enter the "picture" (sign and symbol) of baptism.

Music

There is a sense in which the music itself works theology during congregational singing. The most obvious notion in this regard might be the marriage of text and tune, and mode or tonality as a part of a

---

20 C. Randall Bradley, "Congregational Song as Shaper of Theology: A Contemporary Assessment" in *Review and Expositor, 100* (Summer, 2003): 352.

21 Calvin R. Stapert, *A New Song for an Old World: Musical Thought in the Early Church* (Grand Rapids, MI: Eerdmans Publishing, 2007), 196.

22 John L. Bell, *That Singing Thing: A Case for Congregational Song* (Chicago: GIA Publications, 2000), 59, 65.

23 Hustad, *Jubilate II,* 448.

24 Hustad, *Jubilate II,* 449.

connection to meaning, a sense of *mood* and emotional associations. As previously stated, musicologists and psychologists recognize, "Music does evoke emotions, there is just not evidentiary material to solidly say 'why?'[25] In addition, responses to musical stimuli are not consistent, making any attempts at analysis to be "a very complex area of study … not readable in simple natural science terms." This *not knowing* what gives music its effect itself presents a characteristic ethos of worship as mystery. Jeremy Begbie's work observes the potential for music to advance theological truth through associations such as resolution and salvation, time and dispensation, harmonic congruity and incongruity, improvisation and giving, repetition and Eucharistic living, and so forth.[26] Though congregational song's simplicity may seem not to flesh out all of these, they are at least represented there. In fact, the simplicity itself may represent a theological dynamic.

Music intersects with theological truth and spiritual application at the baptism as experience of the moment joins the song of past, present, and future realities in thought, emotion, kinesis, and audible sounds coming from without and within the worshiper. Repetition, another characteristic of music, provides its dynamic. "It is not sound pattern alone which mean, but people who mean through producing and receiving sound patterns in relation to each other."[27] These applications occur in the moment and space of the stirred water, but also bring past and future, and near and far places into baptism's reality. We sing a *new song*.

Congregational singing provides a meaningful way to involve the whole gathered body in the biblical act of admonishing one another in psalms, hymns, and spiritual songs, making melody in our heart to the Lord, Who is present. Through song and singing, intentional meaning can be tied to the acts of baptism and Lord's Supper, and the significance of the moment, while simultaneously reminding worshipers of their own identity in Christ individually and in community. The singing may provide expression of the mystery of *koinonia* and a sense of the presence that is explained by the residence of the Holy Spirit among us. Members of the body work the aspects of community in which the many members physically and audibly participate as one. The blending of the individual

25 Leonard Meyer, *Emotion and Meaning in Musc* (Chicago: University of Chicago Press, 1956), 12.

26 Jeremy S. Begbie, *Theology, Music, and Time* (Cambridge: Cambridge University Press, 2000), 4–8.

27 Ibid., 13.

voices into one new conglomerate sound proclaims submission to the mission of the church. These dynamics are not "in" and "of" the music itself, but are reflected in its mysterious effect on those who are not only singing it, but hearing it at the same time.

"We have a soteriology of abundance represented in a rhetoric of abundance which in the form of prayer leads us into a spiral of transcendence."[28] In the corporate worship setting, surrounded by the body of believers and in the presence of the Lord Himself, when we are drawn in to the marvelous dynamic symbol and rite of baptism as a new believer is added to the church, and the church and individual are renewed, how can we keep from singing? How can we not be renewed in mission to declare again, "Here is water."?

Special Services

Our life of worship includes rites of passage that occur as part of God's providence of our lives. Our roots of faith are deepened in landmark moments of our lives as we covenant with other believers within the local congregation to remain faithful to vows we have made, or prepare to lay a loved one's body to rest in a service of worship. Weddings, funerals, parent dedications, ordinations, and commissioning services for mission groups are all *rites* of the local church body that encourage faithfulness by marking these special moments in our lives and in our community. Again, congregational singing offers aid to memorable moments when selected, exercised, and integrated as an aspect of these sacred actions.

My father served as a Baptist pastor. The last twenty-five years of his ministry were spent as pastor of Calvary Baptist Church in Jackson, Tennessee. For all those years, he invested his life in the people of Calvary, conducting funerals and weddings, visiting in homes and hospital rooms, counseling and loving these families. His own funeral service was a meaningful tribute to the life he lived, and an expression of confident hope for the life to come. Dad loved to sing. He had a rich baritone voice that he used in worship to hymn the Lord. His memorial service began with the great hymn, "All Hail the Power of Jesus' Name," and concluded with "When We All Get to Heaven." As part of the family, I found it a little difficult to sing through the emotions of loss, but found comfort, hope, and assurance through the stirring sound of the church singing. At one point my mother whispered, "Daddy would have loved this." She

28 David S. Ford, *Self and Salvation,* 113.

was referring to the gathering of people and the spirited singing of the familiar hymns. I answered back, "I think he *is* loving it, Mom." To this day, I sense a closeness to him when singing hymns of praise because I believe that is what he is doing as well. An important part of my faith life is anticipating the day when I will join him to "sing and shout the victory." Reconnecting with loved ones who have left our physical presence is never the focus of Christian worship, but that does not mean worship cannot include a sense of the real involvement of the "great cloud of witnesses." I cannot help but believe that our singing joins our voices to the eternal song that our timeless God must surely hear emanating not just from our voices, but from our hearts. In this singing, we look to what is to come. "O that with yonder sacred throng we at His feet may fall. We'll join the everlasting song and crown Him Lord of all!"

Chapter 8

RENEWED SINGING – RENEWED WORSHIP

> Strip off your oldness; you know a new song. A new person, a New Covenant, a new song. People stuck in the old life have no business with this new song; only those who are new persons can hear it, renewed by grace and throwing off the old, sharers already in the New Covenant, which is the Kingdom of Heaven. All our love yearns toward that, and in its longing our love sings a new song. Let us sing this new song not with our tongues, but with our lives.[1]
>
> –*Augustine*

I have colleagues who have utilized the scriptural admonition to "sing a new song unto the Lord" as a polemic for tossing out music that has been used, and possibly overused, and embracing a new repertoire. To me, the psalmist's "new song" admonition seems best applied to our singing rather than our repertoire. New music has its time and place, but the new song in our worship is surely the reflection of becoming a "new creature" as all things are becoming new (2 Cor. 5:17). Surely you know

1 J. E. Rotelle, ed. *Works of St. Augustine: A Translation for the Twenty-First Century.* (New York: New City Press, 1995), 2000.

the serendipitous joy that catches us by surprise when an old song becomes a new expression of present praise. Of course, the same "aha" can occur with new music. It is the singer and the singing that have become new in the fresh breath of God's Spirit. A William Cowper hymn exclaims, "Sometimes the light surprises the Christian when he sings. It is the Lord that rises with healing in His wings," an especially meaningful lyric from Cowper who battled through life with a proclivity toward a deep, dark depression. Even the spirit of one given to the doldrums can be surprised and made new.

Terry's wife attended our church accompanied by her children week after week. Terry seemed like a nice guy, and treated his wife and children well as far as I could tell, just observing from what little interaction I could see when he drove up to let them off in the parking lot Sundays and Wednesdays. Members of his wife's Sunday school class had been praying for Terry's salvation for quite some time. The only time he attended services were on special occasions like Christmas and Easter, or sometimes for special concerts. The church's pastor made numerous attempts to evangelize Terry through personal visits. Nothing seemed to get through to bring about the visible declaration of faith that evangelicals watch for when an individual responds to an invitation to conversion offered at the end of most services of worship. In Terry's case, concerted efforts of prayer and witness seemed to be falling on deaf ears.

Halfway through the presentation of an Easter Cantata on a Sunday evening, my conducting was distracted by choir members whose attention was focused on something going on behind me as I stood on the conductor's platform. During a half note rest in the score, I heard a low level mumbling taking place behind me. The music segued into a setting of a familiar hymn, "Man of Sorrows' What a Name!" As I turned to invite the congregation's participation in the music, I took advantage to observe what had been distracting the choir singers. There was Terry, kneeling at the altar steps, tears flowing down his face. The congregation's singing was a mixed bag of enthusiastic participation and hushed realization. Before the first stanza reached the repeated frame, "Hallelujah! What a Savior!", Terry's wife and two children had joined him at the altar in an emotional reunion that proclaimed gospel. Soon the pastor and others joined the family and the ring of "Hallelujah! What a Savior!" seemed to gain a volume and intensity that is as difficult to describe as it is impossible to forget. The singing changed from a perfunctory recitation of a song listed in the printed Easter program to an anthem of victory.

At the end of that evening's service, my conceited thinking first turned to the fact that Terry's salvation moment took place during a music presentation, further legitimizing the importance of music's role in the church. That bubble burst when the pastor shared Terry's own reflection on what had taken place in the service. He exclaimed that he did not really know why he responded on this night when he had rejected so many previous opportunities to come to Christ, nor could he really explain how God's Spirit had spoken to his heart. He simply knew that the Lord was calling him to surrender his heart and life. Explaining his timing, he said he did not want to wait until the end of the service. He declared, "I had to make things right, right then." When I reflect back on that occurrence along with many others, I am reminded of what Calvin Miller calls, "the capricious nature of the Holy Spirit."[2] The Gospel reminds us that the wind blows wherever it pleases. "You hear its sound, but you cannot tell where it has come from, or where it is going" (Jn 3:5–8).

From the beginning of this book, we have noted that worship renewal is a gift of the Holy Spirit and thus is something for which we pray, rather than something which we achieve. It is our nature to strive toward something that we perceive as a need. No effective leader sits idly by as their followship sinks into the sea of mediocrity or blows up in explosive destruction or division. I join my voice with others, however, to sound the call that any efforts as leaders, or as followers, toward renewal in worship must come from biblically sound, Spirit-directed, prayer-tested hearts characterized by Christ-like humility. Actions suggested in this chapter, as in others, must be laid before the altar in the prayer closet and in the sanctuary prior to any implementation. No human effort toward renewal in and of itself produces genuine renewal in the hearts of worshipers or in our relationship with God. The numinous activity of God's Spirit will never be manipulated by our actions. Leaders must remain diligent to discern the artificial, lest our worship environments be swept away by the sad game of *masquerade* that characterizes our culture and so easily spills into our churches and their worship.

In this chapter, I would like to consider characteristics of worship that evidence the need for renewal, suggest some actions that may serve that renewal, and consider the results of what a worship might look like if it is undergoing renewal and renewing. I will synthesize suggestions that

---

2 Calvin Miller related the inability to predict the timing of the Spirit in messages shared with Forest Hills Baptist Church, Nashville, TN, during a worship conference in which we served together in 2004.

could serve the purpose of renewal with an obvious special interest toward congregational singing's role as a supportive and motivational activity. I invite you to revisit sacred actions of worship as I will suggest ways leaders might become intentional in worship design that highlight these actions in hopes of helping all worshipers to be intentional with understanding in exercising them. Finally, I will turn attention to the role of leadership in directing congregational worship singing and begin a discussion of congregational singing rehearsals as a possible means of application of the issues outlined in this book.

Sprinkled throughout the discussions of this book, we have noted indicators that worship practice has become anthropocentric in many churches of our day. Sin is powerful, but I am reminded that it has no creation of its own, but rather attaches itself to the good of God's creation. For example, the adversary perverts human perception of sexuality to new uses. Sin is, of necessity, parasitic. In this sense, sin does not seek to destroy worship; rather, it attaches itself to it as if to feed off the power in the things of worship. Because worship can be hijacked, it is crucial to give extensive prayerful consideration to how our worship measures up to biblical mandates, sensibilities, and models. Combining my own reflections and research with the writings of evangelical statesmen for whom I have high respect, I present the following non-exhaustive list of signals that a church's worship needs to be renewed:

Signs that worship needs renewal

1. Worship is focused on human experience
2. Worshipers are passive as spectators
3. Worship lacks a spirit of joy and/or enthusiasm
4. Form and structure of worship liturgy lacks flow or understandability
5. Little or no sense of mystery and awe
6. Singing is dominated by platform performance
7. Preaching is lacking in Gospel focus, enthusiasm, or sense of authenticity
8. The Bible is not central to worship
9. Little or no reading of Scripture apart from the sermon

10. Infrequent observances of ordinances
11. Atmosphere lacks spirit of hospitality and welcome

This list should at least assist leaders in beginning a process of worship evaluation. While it is obvious that many of these signs do not pertain to congregational singing directly, congregational singing is affected by them, and offers affect when addressed toward them. For instance, in #1 above, careful attention to the direction of congregational song language would potentially aid an emphasis to turn worship's focus away from human experience toward a God-centeredness. In each instance where there is indication that worship needs renewal, leaders do well to consider ways congregational singing may provide meaningful assistance.

The list below is intended to assist prayerful church leaders in refocusing worship with activities and emphases that serve the purpose of renewal.

Actions toward renewing worship

1. Leaders emphasize the priority of worship as the one indispensible activity of the church
2. Leaders emphasize worship as an active engagement with God by all worshipers
3. Renewed focus on God's story in the Gospel of Christ as central to worship
4. Renewed commitment to active participation in singing, listening, and serving in worship
5. Renewed commitment to personal worship as preparation for gathered worship
6. Renewed vitality in prayers pointed toward the activity and freedom of the Holy Spirit to act in worship
7. Teaching and preaching on the spiritual and symbolic nature of worship
8. Integration of singing with flow of worship—purposeful singing
9. Congregational singing rehearsals (see chapter 9)
10. Enact opportunities for worship education among church members

11. Renew emphasis on ordinances as acts of worship
12. Utilize printed and electronic communications to aid worship development
13. Leaders emphasize attitudes of worship—humility, teachable spirit, joy, reverence, gratitude, service

The partial list of actions that serve the purpose of worship renewal is further served by consideration as to congregational singing's contribution to each of the actions. Application of these considerations to selection, preparation, and singing of the congregation's song in worship helps steer clear of the kinds of self-serving confusion that comes from a less intentional process.

Characteristics of renewed and renewing worship

1. Worshipers enter the gathering with prepared and tempered expectancy
2. Restored sense of the dramatic nature of worship dialogue—revelation & response
3. Recovered understanding of our ecclesiology, church
4. Display of worshipful attitudes—humility, teachable spirit, joy, reverence
5. Church members display concern for one another above themselves
6. Church members demonstrate a growing concern to evangelism and social outreach
7. Biblical spirituality is heightened
8. A tangible atmosphere of Christian community and hospitality

Common criteria for Christian Worship

1. Biblical
2. Dialogic
3. Covenantal

4. Trinitarian
5. Communal
6. Hospitable
7. "in but not of the world"
8. Generous
9. Evangelistic

Worship Renewal through Singing in the Sacred Actions of Worship

The actions of worship hold deep meaning and intention in the engagement with God we call worship. I want to invite your consideration of sacred actions with a prayerful eye toward renewal. Consider ways that singing our worship as we act can assist our understanding both of what it is we are doing and what it is we are singing. The aforementioned affectations of words and music and their meanings apply and assist attachment in a way that aids human memory and expression both logically and spiritually.

The Gathering

Since worship is all of life, the gathering is a continuation of worship rather than the sum total of what it means to worship. It is not as though when our foot is outside the threshold of the sanctuary we are not worshiping, and then as we step across the threshold of the sanctuary we suddenly begin worshiping. Worship does not begin "at the first note of the prelude" as some worship guides erroneously indicate. We come to gathered worship worshiping. The act of gathering is itself an act of worship expression. The Lord has invited us to worship Him, and has "called us into fellowship with His Son Jesus Christ, our Lord" (1 Cor 1:9). He has admonished us not to "forsake the assembling of ourselves" (Heb 10:24). It is good to encourage our churches to better understand their Saturday before Sunday as a day of worship through preparation. Setting aside time to read selected Scripture, review worship songs, and pray for Sunday's gathering could help prepare worshipers for the Lord's Day gathering and serve as a training ground for our children as they learn the importance and focus of Christian worship.

Leaders often remind people of the importance of Sunday worship attendance and subsequently count nickels and noses to determine the "success" of worship's appeal, but additional steps by these leaders may better demonstrate their commitment to minister in the worship gathering. Leaders can guide church members to understand their own responsibility as ministers to the gathered environment. Providing gathered worship information and material ahead of time to members would seem to encourage the priesthood of the believers in their service of worship. Worship singing can be enhanced by providing access to recorded and printed lyrics and music for the entire congregation as is legally possible.[3] I have attended services where music is being played in the hallways as worshipers enter the building for the gathering. Imagine if such music assisted worshipers to sing their gathering intentions as they "Come Into His House and gather in His Name to worship Him,"[4] or as they "Come into His Presence with thanksgiving in their hearts and give Him praise."[5] Churches that gather small groups during the week or on Sunday prior to full congregational worship would do well to review the songs for gathered worship as opportunity to interpret their meaning, review their biblical foundation, or simply teach worshipers to be better prepared to join in enthusiastic singing as ministry and praise.

Some Ways to Enhance Sunday Singing in Gathered Worship

1. Leaders provide worshipers material to help prepare for gathered worship
    a. Use the church's website to communicate song selections, recorded examples, text, and/or written notation for church members during the week for devotion and personal/family preparations—inform worshipers where worship helps may be located
    b. Provide information where church members can locate recorded and published music for further review. Encourage the purchase of hymnals for every home

3 Online services make more music accessible for download and listening than ever before. In addition there is a trend of music publishers toward providing access through popular outlets as well as through their own internet access. Visit www.ccli.com and www.lifewayworship.com for examples.

4 Text from "We Have Come Into His House" by Bruce Ballinger, *Baptist Hymnal 2008*, #666.

5 Text from "Come Into His Presence" by Lynn Baird, *The Baptist Hymnal 2008*, #584.

c. Teach small group (see chapter 3 on family worship) leaders songs to engage the church in its developing worship language at every level

d. Provide biblical text for sermon, readings, and songs for personal and family review. Indicate connections between sung, read, and preached materials ahead of time

e. Rehearse all congregational music with choir, instrumentalists, and staff weekly

2. Provide music in hallways and on the church grounds that encourages gathering as community of faith, and underscores entrance with thanksgiving

3. Conduct periodic congregational singing rehearsals

The Word

In 2007, I attended a chapel service at Union University to hear a dear friend preach. I had not seen David Platt for a few years and wanted to surprise this young pastor and theologian. David stood to preach and briefly described the scene recorded in Nehemiah 8, when the people requested Ezra to read the Word of the Lord. After a few comments on the centrality of God's Word to worship, David began to quote the first eight chapters of the book of Romans from memory. He had no aids, no props, and no media projection. He was quoting the book verbatim from the NIV translation. Many of the students followed along in their Bibles, as did I. The memorization was an admirable feat, but the longer the recitation went, the more powerful the message of the Word itself became. About the time David began the opening words of Romans 8, "Therefore, there is now no condemnation for those who are in Christ Jesus …," a few students stood in honor of the spoken Word. A few phrases later, more students stood, and within a sentence or two, no one remained seated including my daughter and me. There was a palpable power in the recitation of the Word.

Pastors and worship music leaders must trust the efficacy of the Word. "At no point in our pilgrimage do any Christians mature beyond this ministry so that they can become *self-feeders.*"[6] As with any action of worship, I am not advocating a superstitious waving of the Bible as a magic wand over God's people. On the other hand, I do strongly advocate for corporate worship gatherings a higher level of appreciation for the gift of the revelation of God through our canonized Scripture, the Holy Bible. Asking the congregation to "stand in honor of the reading of God's Word," as is the practice of many churches, seems at the very least to draw attention to the special nature of that which comes from the Bible's pages. Singing that underscores preparation for hearing holds potential to assist those who "have ears to hear" (Lk 14:35). Worship music leaders regularly select music that connects to the theme of the pastor's sermon, a practice that can underscore the Word's application, but a respectful attitude may be further enhanced by singing that indicates a reverence for the very act and/or the fact of the Scriptures itself. In the previous chapter, I noted the new hymn, "Speak, O Lord." Singing this hymn or other worship songs that evoke similar attitudes could serve well the prayer for illumination in free-church environments. Repeating the song weekly just prior to the reading of the Word either for a set number of weeks, or as an ongoing practice, could underscore the need for spiritual preparation and could participate in its accomplishment.

Suggestions for Singing to Enhance Worship through the Word

1. Sing a hymn, psalm, or worship song as preparation to hear the reading or preaching of Scripture—review song indexes for possible selections, or even compose a refrain for repeated use in your setting
2. Sing a response of praise for the reading of God's Word
3. Read scriptural references prior to singing worship songs
4. Draw attention to scriptural allusions within songs to be sung
5. Print and/or project biblical references for activities in worship including singing

6 Michael Horton, *Christless Christianity: The Alternative Gospel of the American Church* (Grand Rapids, MI: Baker Books, 2008), 253.

The Table

The Lord's Supper is the central act of gathered worship in the New Testament. Sadly, Baptists, as other evangelicals, have treated its observance as an optional elective, rather than a needed ingredient that enacts Sunday's message in the lives of the elect while making declaration to those outside the faith. Recent calls to more frequent participation in the ordinance are a well-received means of renewing worship. Attention by worship designers to its observance as a meaningful act is crucial to the execution of renewal efforts, and a strong indicator that leaders are serious about trusting the Lord for the sum and substance of renewing our worship.

"When a church practices baptism and the Lord's Supper, it obeys Christ's teaching and example. In so doing, it portrays Christ's death and resurrection, the testimony of every believer's own spiritual rebirth, as well as the church's collective hope for the final resurrection. These two practices, in short, proclaim the gospel. Thus, even congregations that have long-forsaken biblical doctrine regarding regeneration, Christ's substitutionary death, or the hope of heaven, still proclaim these truths in their liturgies as they reenact these signs." The new birth may be ignored, but baptism portrays it. Christ's atonement may be denied in the sermon, but the Lord's Supper proclaims it. In such cases, tradition at the table speaks more truth than the preaching from the pulpit."[7]

Singing is a powerful means of preparing for worship at the Table, for partaking in its mysteries, and responding to the glory of the Savior it proclaims. Songs that encourage our reflection on Christ's sacrifice, such as "O Sacred Head Now Wounded" can form our approach to reception of the elements of the Supper. New hymns that call attention to our actions through the steps of the Supper are beneficial as well, and can be used one verse at a time to walk worshipers through the reception of the elements and place the worship in a spirit of hope looking to the return of the Savior. "Communion Hymn" by Keith Getty and Stuart Townend serves well in this capacity. The song utilizes composition techniques that enhance the reflective lyrics with appropriate text painting and a memorable melody line. Singing songs reflecting on Christ's broken body either when coming to the Table or while passing the bread of communion among worshipers can certainly enhance understanding and spiritual ethos of our worship. Singing of the new life or new covenant in preparation for drinking new

---

7 Mark Dever "The Church" in *A Theology for the Church,* Daniel Akin, ed. (Nashville: B&H Publishing, 2007), 783.

wine may assist worshipers as they "drink and remember." Too often the phrase, "they sang a hymn and went out" from Matthew 26 is glazed over as a signal to gather our things, get on our coats, and head for the door. Even in environments where the ethos of the Lord's Supper centers on remembering His death, we can surely pause to celebrate the result of His sacrifice and the promise of His return. The Table, after all, projects the promise of the Great Banquet as well as recalls the last moments Jesus spent with His followers before sacrificing His own body and blood. Singing can provide audible evidence to the body that is formed into one only by the work of its Head, Jesus Christ.

Enhancing Worship at the Table through Singing

1. Sing songs of the cross in preparation to observe the Supper
2. Encourage worshipers to direct singing toward the physical table as symbolic gesture during appropriate songs with appropriate lyrics
3. Plan an extended period of singing as response following participation in the Table, including songs of thanksgiving, praise, fellowship, and hope
4. Utilize media projection to accentuate aspects of the Supper's effect, such as biblical period dramatizations, photos of church members in fellowship and ministry, or cultural signs that point to the eminent return of Christ

Sending

The closing of gathered worship is an oft-overlooked action of worship. Refocus of worshipers' attention to the fact of life as worshipers cannot only assist the ending of our gathering time, but may well strengthen the work of ministry by the church that departs to live in, but not of the world as ambassadors for Christ. Singing as the last activity of gathered worship not only reflects the model we see at the end of the last Supper, but also places song on the mind of worshipers as they depart the sanctuary of gathered worship. Music holds power to assist memory, and can surely reinforce the teaching and proclamation that has taken place in our gathering on a given Sunday.

Enhancements for Singing our Sending

1. Sing a song of departure—check indexes for hymns, songs, or psalms, or compose a song of commission
2. Repeat a song or refrain from an earlier part of the gathered worship liturgy for the day—consider a song that calls for specific action
3. Sing a benedictory prayer as a body gathered that prepares to go out and fulfill mission
4. Sing a fellowship song that reminds worshipers of their connectedness even as they part

Baptism

Baptism may well be the most underestimated action of worship, as it visually proclaims the power of the Gospel to conquer sin and death and to resurrect fallen humanity to walk in new life. I am amazed that many churches minimize this teaching of Jesus by marginalizing its practice to a position of a service "add on." Even though my denomination takes its name from this practice and assesses a church's success by the number of those who undergo baptism in a year, there is still a deficit in its practice in many church settings. Even many churches who call themselves evangelistic ignore the potential of the testimony dramatized in baptism to demonstrate Gospel power. Singing can assist our correction of a tendency to underplay baptism as worship action.

Enhancing Worship through Baptism by Singing

1. Sing songs of salvation in preparation for baptism
2. Sing song phrases or refrains that reflect each action of baptism: death, burial, resurrection, living a new way
3. Sing a hymn or worship song that identifies the entrance of the candidate into the fellowship of the church
4. Sing songs of praise in response following baptism
5. Fashion an entire worship service around the baptism of new believers

6. Encourage worshipers to recall their own baptisms and sing familiar songs as underscore

Weddings, Funerals, Dedications, and Commissions

Churches are cultural venues of choice for several life rituals. Wise leaders recognize and protect the church's integrity in offering space and ministerial services, especially to non-believers who seek a conducive environment for a ceremonial event without attachment of faith practice. Pastors and worship leaders are gate protectors relative to activities and rites that, at heart, are sacred worship. One way of solidifying witness as a congregation is for a congregation to faithfully attend and minister as singing ministers during special services of worship such as weddings and funerals. As autonomous entities in Baptist polity, local churches maintain different practices relative to ordinations and dedications. Careful teaching relative to these worship practices can aid understanding and expectation by church members and community. Congregational singing as ministry function may aid this teaching by deepening such understandings through practice.

Enhancing weddings, funerals, commissions, dedications by congregational singing

1. Sing songs appropriate to the worship action addressed—songs of hope and Gospel at a funeral, songs of prayer at a wedding, songs of commitment and promise at dedications
2. Provide memorable printed copies of lyrics to individuals and families who are the object of special ministries
3. Enlist and train singers to serve in special ministry situations
4. Utilize sung music during entrance and departure of special services that reflect ministry actions such as memorializing, uniting in marriage, dedicating parents or children, or commissioning persons to special mission
5. Video record messages and singing connected to special service worship actions, such as personal testimonials, songs of inspiration

Pastoral Leadership of Congregational Singing

If worshipers are to consider others as better than themselves and approach worship in such a way as prioritizes the work of the Holy Spirit among them, they need leaders who lead in a pastoral manner. To foster an atmosphere where worshipers serve Christ by ministering to one another and demonstrate a desire to reach the world they have been called to reconcile, then it is my contention that congregational singing should be led in a pastoral manner.

Being Pastoral

John Witvliet says that a "pastoral worship leader loves the truth of the Christian gospel" and that they will do what it takes to "hone their pastoral sensibilities." He goes on to say, "They know the names, faces, and stories of people in the congregation."[8] This same nature is affirmed by Eugene Peterson's characterization, "Pastoral work is that aspect of Christian ministry that specializes in the ordinary." [9] It appears, then, that a "pastoral manner" reflects a sensitivity to God and His Word and to the needs of people in the ordinary, great or small. Leading congregational singing that encourages ministry among God's people assumes an understanding of who these people are, including those with particular needs, as well as those with particular giftedness to minister.

I have heard numerous worship leaders talk about their desire to demonstrate their personal connection with the Lord in worship as a demonstration to others. In a desire to model what it looks like and sounds like (assuming you have a microphone) to be in touch with the Spirit, I am afraid they have overlooked the real heart of congregational singing's witness that comes when men and women and boys and girls in the pews are singing with head and heart engaged. The worship leader whose eyes are closed, working to evidence a special connection, cannot possibly see the grandmother pointing through the lines of the hymn teaching her grandson to follow notes and words in singing worship. The spirited participation of a dad struggling with relationships but proclaiming God's grace before his family, may be lost to the guitar player whose attention is focused on the monitor levels of his Aviom.

---

8 John Witvliet, *Worship Seeking Understanding,* 283.

9 Eugene H. Peterson, *Five Smooth Stones for Pastoral Work,* (Grand Rapids, MI: Eerdmans Publishing, 1992), 1.

Leaders, it is time that we raise our heads, recognize, and celebrate the presence of the gathered body of Christ! It is time we minister to one another as we worship in spirit and truth. It is time we still the overpowering accompaniment, so that we might hear the resonant voice of fellow believers struggling to balance lament and exuberance. Making eye contact with the worshipers we seek to lead, we need to inspire worshipers to utilize their gifts to admonish one another and spur one another on to good works. A genuine sensitivity to the ministry among the people gives guidance to next steps for the leader in developing the worshiping community in its singing.

If our concern is to encourage worshipers in their ministry to pastoral needs through song, it seems the worship music leader would need to trust the process of worship as ministry. In corporate worship, this would imply having faith in God's work in and through the liturgy, *leitourgia,* "the work, or service, of the people," and understanding the pastoral nature and nurture of corporate worship in order to offer leadership that encourages the congregation in its ministry among its members.[10] Jesuit J. A. Jungmann has reminded, "... for centuries the liturgy, actively celebrated, has been the most important form for pastoral care."[11] John Witvliet says that the gathered community of faith engaged in the liturgy of worship presents formidable characteristics of spiritual possibility. In fact, he reminds us that "discernment happens best in community."[12] As worship leader, the musician has opportunity to increase awareness among worshipers of the incarnation by directing thought and activity (such as singing) in its light. If Witvliet is correct, the potential for discernment relative to the needs of worshipers and presence of Christ in their midst would seem to present the basic tenets for ministry to take place in and through the congregation. Terry York and David Bolin point out, "The shepherd must call forth the poet/prophet that exists in the soul and giftedness of each member and in the soul and giftedness of the congregation as a whole. It has to

10 Hustad, *Jubilate II,* 316–317. Hustad positions evangelical worshipers as typically nonliturgical, but as always having a script that gives form to their worship; in essence a liturgy with a set of *essential actions.*

11 Willimon, *Worship as Pastoral Care,* 35. Willimon quotes from J. A. Jungmann, *Pastoral Liturgy* (New York: Herder and Herder, 1962), 380.

12 John D. Witvliet, *Worship Seeking Understanding: Windows Into Christian Practice,* (Grand Rapids, MI: Baker Academic, 2003), 272.

do with a spiritual understanding of the life and work of the worshiping community."[13]

A pastor has responsibility to call attention to what takes place in the worship event beyond the scripting. Spiritual ignition, love between members of the faith community, and comfort and conviction stirred in the hearts of worshipers are all mysterious energies which occur regularly, though unpredictably, in gathered worship. Calvin Johansson says, "… music is the most logical of all the arts to deal with mystery."[14] Paul Westermeyer points out, "That God, the source and ground of the whole universe, should take flesh among us and care for all of us is irrational, beyond comprehension, alien. The song will obviously reflect this reality."[15] Plantinga and Rozeboom say of our oneness in Christ, "This can be accomplished only by, in, and through the Holy Spirit."[16] Randall Bradley reminds us that as we conduct ministry, "… one must realize that providing Christ's presence is the ultimate goal."[17] This would imply that a characteristic of leading in a pastoral manner for a worship music leader would be a humble spirit, allowing the work of worship to minister through the song and singing of the people as the Spirit of God moves and speaks through the song sung by those in whom He resides. The pastoral leader seeking to retain worship's focus on Christ's work will surely guide attention to the Spirit's work and presence in all aspects of gathered worship.

Discerning Pastoral Needs

In order to point the congregational song toward pastoral concerns, it is logical to assume the worship music leader may need some systematic means of considering what those concerns may be. A church's published prayer list of bereaved and ill may provide a beginning point for discernment, but

---

13 Terry w. York and C. David Bolin, *The Voice of Your Congregation: Seeking and Celebrating God's Song for Us,* (Nashville: Abingdon Press, 2005), 32–33.

14 Calvin Johansson, *Music & Ministry: A Biblical Counterpoint,* (Peabody, MA: Hendrickson Publishers, 1984), 91.

15 Paul Westermeyer, "Here, Now, and Beyond," *The Hymn*, Vol. 54, No. 1, (January 2003), 15.

16 Plantinga and Rozeboom *Discerning the Spirits,* 102.

17 Randall Bradley, *From Postlude to Prelude: Music Ministry's Other Six Days* (St. Louis: Morningstar Music Publishers, 2004), 283. Although Bradley is talking specifically about visitation ministry of the music minister, the same manner and demeanor applies to ministry in the worship event.

not delve into those concerns more private in nature which may remain unarticulated, or may not expand to include more global concerns.

In many evangelical "nonliturgical" churches, a segment of the worship is provided for "pastoral prayer." Don Hustad concludes, "that title ('pastoral prayer') encourages misunderstanding of the congregation's role in worship. In historical (and much modern) worship, it is correctly listed as 'Prayers of the Faithful' (baptized believers) or 'Prayers of the People' and is understood to be spoken on their behalf by the officiating minister."[18] In *The Worship Resource Book,* in similar fashion to *The Book of Common Prayer,* "Prayers of the People" are enumerated categorically as "Topics for Petitions" based upon the historic form. Utilization of this listing might serve as reminder to the worship leader as he or she is planning congregational song for worship, heightening awareness of pastoral concerns through prayers "For the Creation, For the World, For the Nation, For the Local Community, For the Worldwide Church, For the Local Church, For those with Special Needs."[19] This seems fertile soil for helping the worship leader to consider what concerns might be on the hearts of worshipers, and for helping worshipers pray the songs they sing. Song and singing has historically been connected closely to prayer. In discussing singing's infrequent reference from the New Testament, Michael Hawn has noted, "Singing may have been referenced rarely because it was assumed that when one prayed, one also sang."[20]

Selecting Material

Witvliet confronts us with the fact, "As worship leaders, we have the important and terrifying task of placing words of prayer on people's lips. It happens every time we choose a song and write a prayer." [21] The selection of material that is scripturally sound, appropriate, attainable, singable, and generally usable within the language of the congregation is further complicated by its need to function at multiple levels. Wren reminds us of a question to be asked, "Can people of different generations, cultures, and circumstances find themselves in these words?"[22] Regardless

18 Don Hustad, *Jubilate II,* 323.

19 *The Worship Sourcebook,* (Grand Rapids, MI: Calvin Institute of Christian Worship, 2004), (Grand Rapids, MI: Faith Alive Christian Resources, 2004), (Grand Rapids, MI: Baker Books, 2004), 182–184.

20 C. Michael Hawn, "Sung Prayer," in *Discerning the Spirits,* 147.

21 Witvliet, *Worship Seeking Understanding,* 282.

22 Wren, *Praying Twice,* 184.

of the motivation for song inclusion initially, ministry would be served by reconsideration of their inclusion through a pastoral needs lens, remaining sensitive to that application in the singing itself. The context of multiple needs must be considered, lest textual sensitivity be lost.

Theological appropriateness of material selected in address of pastoral concerns would seem a high priority for genuine effectiveness in worship. Gary Furr and Milburn Price remind us that the congregational song gives opportunity for congregational confession and faith expression, and that selection of this material may call for theological address by the preaching pastor or by the worship leader.[23] Brian Wren recognizes that a "hymn poet cannot do systematic theology" and therefore a partnership can be utilized between sermon and song.[24] This would imply that theological interpretation may be necessary in the application of song.

Pastoral concerns likely occur on multiple levels simultaneously. Andrew Lester points out that in pastoral care "what has gone before and what is anticipated are relevant to the present moment."[25] This implies that immediate past, and/or anticipated need weigh upon the worshiper. A national or world calamity such as the events of September 11, 2001, in the U.S., or the Indian Ocean tsunami in 2004, the Katrina hurricane, or earthquake in Haiti would obviously call for address in the congregation's worship, as would a pending war or other calamity. Inclusion of songs of lament, and/or of faith in response to these large scale concerns would also seem to offer ministry to concerns affecting smaller groups or individuals, either personalized within the larger catastrophe or separate altogether. Wren, addressing lament, reminds us, "Lyric should be clear in meaning and open to multiple significance." [26] Material selected for one purpose may serve many.

Leading the Congregational Song

Authentic presentation as a leader in worship is crucial to engagement in congregational song. People do not yield to mere "facts." They respond to a person.[27] Calvin Johannson points out, "When trust exists between

23 Furr and Price, *The Dialogue of Worship*, 51.

24 Brian Wren, "Telling the Truth through Tearful Song," *Journal for Preachers, 26*, 22–36.

25 Andrew D. Lester, *Hope in Pastoral Care and Counseling*, (Louisville, KY: John Knox Westminster Press, 1995), 14.

26 Brian Wren, "Telling the Truth through Tearful Song," *Journal for Preachers 26.02*, (Lent 2003), 22.

27 William Willimon, *Worship as Pastoral Care*, 96.

musician and people a mutually beneficial relationship results. The music director nurtures the congregation, and the congregation responds affirmatively to that nurture."[28] While music performance can carry a certain level of emotionally engaging dynamic, and this reality poses specific dangers, it is trust built on genuine pastoral care that lays groundwork for ministry.

The pastoral musician in his or her leading role serves to prepare the congregation for context and meaning of song and its expression. Often it is assumed that the congregation can appropriate the message and ministry of the song "immediately and without preparation." Brian Wren points out how this can be counterproductive to the ministering environment. For instance, in the case of lament, "… many tearful songs are too particular, or too demanding, to be used without explanation." [29] Practices of tossing up too many songs, repeated too many times, and with little or no explanation, but rather depending on the musical "power" of driving rhythms or resounding organ to carry meaning may work against building of trust, a sense of ethos, and community. It takes a sensitive spirit to open for numinous moments and for ministry, while understanding the level to which the congregation is capable of responding. As Terry York and David Bolin state, "The congregation cannot be made to sing, but they can be invited to enter the stage of growth for which they are ready."[30]

In leading congregational song, the pastoral musician serves as a model toward pastoral care. John Ferguson observes, "It is a duty and delight of the leader of congregational song to energize worshipers in it."[31] This hospitable spirit as a shepherding agent encourages follow-ship and imitation in the very best sense of the word, and nurtures more than the act of singing, but the spirit of ministry and reflection of concern that is the heart of pastoral ministry. Drawing attention to song text, Scriptural association, and application with sensitivity to pastoral needs and concerns fosters the same within the congregation as they sing. This is not just a social grace, but assists the congregation in understanding its commonness in need. Congregational song as ministry welcomes the stranger and encourages invitation into the worship conversation with God precisely in light of needs, and that in awareness of "so great a cloud of

28 Calvin Johannson, *Discipling Music Ministry,* (Peabody, MA: Hendrickson Publishers, 1992), 4.

29 Brian Wren, "Telling Truth Through Tearful Songs," 22.

30 York and Bolin, *The Voice of Our Congregation,* 91.

31 John Ferguson, "Hospitable Leadership for Worship" in *Discerning the Spirits,* 117.

witnesses." "Being aware of the cloud of witnesses means praying for the needs of believers whose plight seems not to touch our own, always aware that when one part of the body suffers, the whole body suffers with it."[32]

Some Conclusions For Pastoral Worship Leaders

The dynamics of congregational song include all the complexities of the meaning of music itself, the understood biblical command and model for its practice, the multiplied dimensions of its meaning and significance, and its effect of group participation and ministry within the worshiping community. As such, there is still much that is mysterious about its effect upon worshipers and worship. Precisely because of its potentially strong and often mysterious effect, worship singing presents opportunity for ministry of the Holy Spirit working in and through those who participate in its expression, and as such, through the song itself to provide effective ministry to pastoral needs and concerns.

We have concluded that a pastoral approach to planning and leading congregational song includes disciplines and sensibilities consistent with what it means to be a pastor who cares about pastoral needs and concerns and who desires to equip the saints for ministry in response to those needs. These sensibilities include the ministry through the song and singing of the faith community. We have come to understand that methodology of addressing congregational song may take many paths, especially in free-church worship, but that a pastoral approach will express a faith in God's engagement in the worship among His people in their ministry of worship, and will determine a method that seeks to empower that ministry rather than getting in its way.

The pastor and worship music leader team must work together in providing pastoral leadership if congregational singing is to reach its full potential to aid worship renewal. A healthy relationship of mutual appreciation and genuine care between these two leaders serves as a model of mutual ministry sharing and receiving. This is precisely the kind of interaction that is being sought among church members in the gathered worship setting. The ability of these two leaders to pray for one another, sing ministry to one another, and receive the ministry extended by one another will go a long way to showing all members of the congregation how to do the same in the worship setting.

32 Ibid., 121.

Congregational Singing Rehearsal – Renewed Singing

One of the dilemmas of worship action in the church is a lack of sufficient time for worship preparation. Congregation members fully expect the pastor to spend time preparing the sermon for preaching and to give appropriate attention to the total atmosphere of gathered Sunday worship. Likewise, the worship music leader is expected to select music carefully and to rehearse personally, as well as preparing to share leadership with fellow musicians of the choir, worship band, and other instrumentalists. Even when these persons are full-time staff members of a local church they may find it difficult to put in enough hours to feel that everything is "ready" for a given Sunday worship time. Nevertheless, church members expect a level of competency by their leaders.

The real dilemma in worship preparation, though, goes beyond the responsibilities of the leaders. The truth is that all worshipers have a responsibility in the gathered worship setting. One of our severe misgivings in present day church practice is that worship is "for the members." That is to say that we assume the members are to be pleased and satisfied with what is done for them or to them in worship gatherings. Another misgiving is that worship is "for the visitors," in hopes the presentation of leaders will draw the visitor to membership. In fact, worship is an engagement with God for His glory on His terms and accomplished only in His way. Worship is the responsibility and delight of every believer. It only seems logical that with this responsibility comes a need for preparation. A church is not likely to experience genuine renewal of its worship environment until concerted effort and emotional energy are given to make proper preparation for short-term and long-term change. Changing actions on part of the pastor and worship music leader will not fundamentally change the worship environment of the church. There must be a redirection in the lives and intentions of the congregation. The church must again take its place in its ministry among its own members and reclaim its role as salt and light in the world, acting as priest to the lost and needy of the community and world.

I am a strong proponent of a concerted worship renewal focus for a specified period of time in the church to serve as a beginning point for reformation of the church's worship. Whether through a protracted series of Sundays where preaching and teaching centers around actions and attitudes of worship, or a weekend focus is utilized to serve as revival, something needs to declare a beginning for changes in the worship atmosphere of the church. Extended prayer emphasis and engagement of all leadership are only appropriate to accompany an effort that will fundamentally change how the church gathers with its head, the Lord Christ, in its times of repositioning its perspective of bowed humility and offering of life to the Lord.

Since congregational singing is a large part of what the church does in its worship and serves as the one point of every service when all worshipers are invited to vocally participate in the worship, I encourage leaders to include a congregational singing rehearsal in any effort toward renewal. The rehearsal is important to the spirit and effect of a worship renewal emphasis on two primary levels. First of all, a rehearsal provides the kind of atmosphere where members share a common vulnerability and exposure of something as personal as their own voice to their fellow church family members. For the talented singers, this surrender demonstrates their offering of the talents with which they have been entrusted in the shared life of the congregation as a body and as ministry in the individual lives of other members of the family. For uncertain singers who may even feel they cannot sing, the surrender demonstrates their willingness to sacrifice vanity for the work of the kingdom and common service to proclaim, praise, and serve. Inability to stir these covenantal attitudes that result in a congregational rehearsal may indicate deeper problems in the spiritual condition of the church. Secondly, a rehearsal provides the immediate laboratory to demonstrate the very attitudes and ministries needed for the weekly worship environment.

The next chapter will outline a rehearsal format that can be adjusted according to the individual church for which a rehearsal would be designed. Supported by fervent prayer and proper leadership preparations, and committed attendance by a significant percentage of the church's membership, the congregational rehearsal may be the single most important event in a focus of worship renewal.

Chapter 9
REHEARSAL FOR SINGING

My grandfather was a strong influence in my life. I spent many summertime hours riding with him in his pickup truck going back and forth to his farms, driving to the farmers' co-op to pick up feed, or just bumping around the pasture, either checking on the herd of cattle or hauling hay. Grandpa liked to fill those moments with either telling me stories from his life, making me laugh with his jokes, or singing. When his choice was the latter, I never knew whether the song would be a nonsensical song he learned in his childhood or if it would be a favorite hymn. I usually had no warning. We might be driving along for an hour with no words spoken, and suddenly the hum of the road noise would be broken by Grandpa bursting into one of these recitations, whether poetry or song. I recall that his hymns would sometimes fool me as I would expect to hear the melody all the way through, but since Grandpa was a tenor, he may well float on up to the tenor part. That effect only became musically satisfying as I grew a little older and realized I could provide the melody and we would be rolling across Missouri's highway 63, windows down, proclaiming our faith through a baritone/tenor duet.

On rare occasions, Grandpa would stumble on a word in a song, and would say, "Maybe I better stick to the songs I know by heart." He would also ask me from time to time if I knew a particular hymn "by heart." I knew then, and certainly know now, that he was referring to whether or not I could sing the song from memory. He would sometimes commend a certain song to me by saying, "You might want to learn to sing that one 'by heart.'" That expression, which we might consider old fashioned, presents an important challenge to our worship singing. In our day of words on screens, delivered in six to eight word bites, it concerns me that there may be very few songs that our congregations can sing together "by heart." There is an obvious duplicate meaning in that phrase that should capture our attention as well. An important question for worship leaders in music selection, as well as in how music is sung in worship might be "Can we sing this song by heart?" The duplicate meaning, of course, implies on the one hand whether we have the song memorized, such that we can sing it without the lyrics on the screen or use of a hymnal, and on the other hand, whether we can mean the song from our hearts.

In some ways, these ideas may be complimentary. In our age of entertainment obsession, novelty is far too often a high value that spills into our worship planning and practice. I often hear a similar complaint from two sides of the so-called worship wars. One side says, "We are tired of singing the same old hymns over and over." The other side says, "We do not want to sing those 'seven-eleven' songs over and over again." The fact is that an important aspect of our worship is repetition. We are, in fact, repeating God's story over and over again every week. The Gospel must be central to our weekly gatherings. Repetitions of Scripture, prayer, and yes, song, are only meaningless when we are so disengaged or ill-prepared that we do not mean them. I am convinced that we need enough repetition of songs to be able to sing them into meaning. I am sometimes frustrated by how quickly a song goes by when its message is deeply profound and needs some unpacking. Recently, our Tennessee Men's Chorale sang a song that was new to many of the singers, "Come, People of the Risen King," by Keith & Kristyn Getty. Our rehearsal time was just enough to get the flavor and general sense of this great admonishment to "let every tongue rejoice!" It did not provide us enough time to dig deeply into what it means to call "young and old from every land, men and women of the faith" to a time of rejoicing as "one heart, one voice." Yet, even in our first presentations of this "new" song, I could anticipate that this will be a song we will want to repeat in numerous occasions of worship. I know our group enough to know that we will sing into its meaning more and more over numerous repetitions. I cannot help but believe that, like Grandpa's admonition, this will be one of those songs "you might want to learn to sing by heart."

Worship music leaders, are you giving your congregation and choir songs to sing by heart? Are you challenging teenagers to grow into singing ancient hymns and gospel songs by heart? Are you challenging your senior adults to engage in the repetition of choruses by using them to express their meaning by heart? Are you committed to lead your congregation to know songs at a much deeper level than the drone mantras that far too often serve only as a utility of flow or transition for bored consumers of worship? Do you recognize your responsibility to select music that is worth learning to sing by heart? I am convinced that music chosen simply to get from one mood to the other has no place in sacred worship. Music worth learning to sing by heart should help speak the process of authentic worship that confesses our sin, cries our prayers, lifts our praise, proclaims the Truth, and engages our spirits in concert with the Holy Spirit.

Since I no longer serve regularly in full-time ministry as a local church worship music leader, people often ask me what I miss most about the local church setting. I do not have to ponder on that one. I miss the weekly rehearsal with the church choir(s). There is nothing more gratifying than working to perfect music that expresses our faith, praise, and worship. I love the agogic moment when someone in the choir "gets it;" when repetition of words and music finds its effect working the meaning of words into the mind and heart of one of the singers, or better yet, into the whole chorus. All that work on breath control, posture, and proper diction translates into singing phrases with authentic meaningful expression. Hammering out notes of individual choir parts converts into harmonic coloring of musical nuance that allows musical expression to convey its dramatic meaning. Repeating the rhythms of simple or complicated patterns allows music's punch to come alive and mean more to the singers and those to whom they will present their song. It is an exciting metamorphosis that occurs in weekly choir rehearsals, and it is fulfilling to help guide those experiences that give the choir singers the confidence needed to effectively present their ministry in Sunday worship.

Over years of working weekly choir rehearsals and then standing before congregations in Sunday worship, I have often noted that the choir receives its own ministry at the same time it offers it to others through their singing. No doubt the choir is able to internalize the message of their singing much more than the congregation that hears it is able to do in one hearing. After all, the choir has been working on singing the songs for six weeks and has approached them from every possible musical angle in the process. Through the work of rehearsal, the message has a way of seeping into the soul. I have often said that the choir gets more out of their music than the congregation ever will. So the thought occurs to me, why don't we rehearse the congregation? Why not give the church the same depth of exposure to text and tune? Why not work on singing phrases in a way that helps worshipers who are singing to mean the thought?

The text of some hymns and worship songs use poetic language that is not easily absorbed on the first pass through singing it. Worshipers can be easily distracted trying to recall or learn the melody while the profound nature of a worship song lyric elusively passes them by. Why not give the congregation some of the same repetitious exposure to songs they are asked to use to express their faith and worship as we do the choir? Would worshipers and our worship not benefit from a richer comprehension and preparation for singing out the deep expressions within their hearts? Like the choir, learning the mechanics of balance and blend might help worshipers discover new appreciation for one another in community, as well as becoming more proficient at singing their own part in the church's song. I am a big proponent of the congregational rehearsal, and scheduling them on a regular, periodic basis.

What Does a Congregational Rehearsal Look Like?

The pattern of a congregational rehearsal is much like the structure of a choir rehearsal. For the rehearsal to be beneficial, the leader and accompanists must be well prepared musically and spiritually to guide the experience. The basic components of a rehearsal are included in the following outline:

Warm-up

While technical vocalises probably will not prove effective with a congregation of novice singers, it is important to gain the attention of participants to the idea that the primary activity of a rehearsal is singing. I personally like to use familiar fun songs, or simple vocalises to accomplish this task. Over-dramatizing of such lighthearted fare as "Do, a Dear" from *Sound of Music,* or repetition of very simple scales allows for the establishment of an atmosphere of fun and appropriate playfulness. Another useful tool may be rounds such as "Row, Row, Row Your Boat," especially if part singing will be part of the rehearsal's activity. I have used everything from a school fight song ("Rocky Top" works pretty well in Tennessee) to a children's nursery rhyme ("Twinkle, Twinkle Little Star"). While simple faith songs could certainly be used for warming up the voice, I personally tend toward music that begins singers' concentration on the mechanics of singing apart from the significance of worship expression. Combining some fun singing with simple breathing exercises, posture checks, and stretching exercises should establish the kind of fellowship atmosphere conducive to a congregational rehearsal that can quickly turn its attention to the importance and meaning of singing worship and witness together, and quickly combine that attitude with a posture that indicates something of what we think of God as we sing worship.

Prayer and Preparation

Surprisingly, some members of the congregation may have no idea how deeply spiritual the experience of singing faith can be. I have known church members who, after visiting a choir rehearsal, have been shocked to find out the level at which the choir prays together, understands its ministry responsibility, and studies its message before presenting music for worship. An important aspect of a congregational singing rehearsal will be the connection of singing with the act of communicating with God. Brian Wren joins Augustine in reminding us, "Whoever sings [in worship to God] prays twice."[1] A congregational singing rehearsal needs to begin and end with a time of commitment in prayer. After all, our work is not only preparation for worship, but is in itself an act of worship. It is important to offer this sacrifice of praise preparation to the Lord whose presence we seek among us and whose pleasure is the object of our efforts. This time of prayer is an opportunity for the senior pastor to demonstrate both his pastoral confirmation of the rehearsal activity and his support and encouragement toward the congregation's responsibility of vocal participation in corporate worship.

A part of the prayer time should include teaching about the biblical admonition to sing worship. A study of passages such as those noted in

1 Brian Wren, *Praying Twice: The Music and Words of Congregational Song* (Louisville, KY: Westminster John Knox Press, 2000), 1.

chapter two of this book should aid worshipers in comprehending the serious nature of the enterprise of singing our worship.

Repertoire and Approach

The song list for a congregational rehearsal can come from one of a few approaches. One idea is to include songs that are planned for the next several weeks' worship gatherings. The advantage to this approach is that the application of the music preparation will be made in a short period of time. This is the same principal as many use in a choir rehearsal philosophy. As such, songs that will be included in the coming Sunday's worship order may deserve the most extended amount of rehearsal time. Some attention should be given to songs that will be used in coming services that are new to the congregation. Combining the congregational rehearsal experience with other noted means of exposure may allow the kind of confidence in singing participation that helps get even new songs into the congregation's language of worship expression quickly. Worshipers will likely appreciate the opportunity to be better prepared for these new songs when they appear in worship. Leaders may experience less resistance to new music when the congregation has this chance to make the songs familiar before they are asked to express them as worship. Introducing new songs by addressing the role they will play in the worship dialogue may also encourage their acceptance. While the congregational rehearsal provides opportunity for learning new songs, care should be taken to balance the rehearsal with familiar music that allows the congregation to dig deeper into things they know as well as learn new songs.

Rehearsal Techniques

Obviously, rehearsal of music begins with the simplest hearing and repeating of the music of the songs included in the rehearsal. Building the confidence of singers begins with confirmation that they know the aural and vocal experience of hearing and singing the music. This outer layer of rehearsing may do much to prepare the congregation to engage in singing as worship. Leaders should use their musical judgment as to the amount of repetition needed to simply get the song into the voice of the congregation. Techniques for this process will largely be determined as to whether the song is brand new or if it is either a familiar tune or a song that has very familiar form, verses a brand new song with tricky rhythms or challenging melodic skips. Leaders may want to attempt music familiarization on neutral syllables, such as "la," prior to adding the lyric to the singing. One rehearsal philosophy is to break the music down to the basic components, help singers learn one component at a time and begin to reconstruct the components as the song is learned. The process follows the pattern of a good choir rehearsal. Every repetition moves the singers a step closer to making the song their own.

Within the rehearsal process, every step of progress should be accompanied by explanation of the meaning and intention of the song lyric and music as applied to the worship environment. This technique helps singers to discover meaning, not only of the song, but of the worship process itself. While rehearsing the reflective text of "When I Survey the Wondrous Cross," singers may sense the appropriate marriage of the text and music of HAMBURG the hymn tune most often used with the Isaac Watts text. They may also consider the contemplative character of the tune and associate its appropriateness for approaching the Table of the Lord's Supper. Leaders who can interpret hymn construction techniques can add to the comprehension and subsequent usage of the music when it is actually used in worship. For example, the hymn "When I Survey the Wondrous Cross" makes masterful use of anadiplosis, a poetic technique that uses the last word or idea of a stanza to introduce the beginning thought of the next stanza. The word, "pride" at the end of stanza one prepares for the first phrase of stanza two, "forbid it Lord that I should boast …" Rehearsing the last phrase of one and moving to the next stanza may unearth renewed intensity in the singing.

As with any good choir rehearsal, the congregational rehearsal should avail singers of deeper understanding of text and compositional techniques that lift the meaning of the text to a level of personal and corporate expression. Repeating and rehearsing phrases such that lyrics make more sense can help members in their understanding of how the lyrics are intended to express worship at the same time they are learning to sing with more meaning. A positive consequence of the repetition is that these words tend to stay in the mind of the singers after they leave the rehearsal setting. When the words and music reappear in the flow of worship, they may come as welcome friends ready to help convey the heart of revelation and response. An example of a great hymn that demonstrates the revelation and response form is "Man of Sorrows, What a Name!" Each verse declares a revelation of Christ and His work to which the worshipers respond, "Hallelujah! What a Savior!" Working on this last phrase first and encouraging an enthusiasm in that declaration of His greatness can prepare the congregation to sing with understanding as the apostle Paul has encouraged us to do. I have experienced this song in traditional and contemporary settings as a renewed expression of vibrant worship following a simple rehearsal exercise.

Though the length of the rehearsal may limit interaction, it is often beneficial to give time for limited questions from the congregation, which can help to clarify song meanings and usage for worshipers. In all of these procedures, church members are given the chance to understand that the responsibility for corporate worship is theirs, individually and collectively. The rehearsal gives pastor and worship music leader grand opportunity to advance worship education while preparing this congregational choir to worship with renewed head and heart in the next worship gathering.

Closing of Rehearsal

As with a choir, it may be helpful to sing through Sunday's music at the end of rehearsal, encouraging singers to integrate all that has been learned during the rehearsal. Talking through their placement and function in the service may again assist singers to feel knowledgeable, better understand the meaning of each song and sing it accordingly, and feel a part of the worship team as a contributing member of the faith community. It is also a good opportunity to point out phrases that may bear witness to the Gospel, affording the church its opportunity to share Christ in worship with any who may gather with them on Sunday who are not believers. After singing through Sunday's congregational songs, a time of prayer asking the Lord's presence and power to be upon Sunday's worship would seem appropriate. Appropriate prayer songs might be used either as a part of the closing prayer session, or as a means of completing the dedication aimed at committing the congregation's song to the Lord.

I would encourage leaders to remain sensitive to the Holy Spirit, of course, through the rehearsal. You never know when the work of rehearsal may evolve into a dynamic time of praise expression. I will not forget one church whose pastor opposed the use of contemporary choruses, yet following a rehearsal when the worship music leader unpacked the worship value of Chris Tomlin's "How Great Is Our God," the pastor requested that the evening end with repetition of that very song. The congregation sensed the break-through this singing represented and the singing became a celebration of restoration, renewal, and our great God Himself!

Brian Wren points to the hallmarks of congregational singing. He states, "Singing together brings us together. As we sing together we belong to one another in song. We agree, in effect, not to be soloists, self-absorbed mediators, or competitors, but to compromise with each other, join our voices as if joining hands, listen to each other, keep the same tempo, and thus love each other in the act of singing. For the congregation its song makes a theological statement, 'We are the body of Christ.'"[2] Rehearsing our song and singing gives wonderful opportunity to prepare spiritually for all aspects of gathered worship and to place a song in the mind and heart of worshipers.

Sample Congregational Rehearsal Order

Opening remarks – "The apostle Paul appeals to us to offer our bodies as living sacrifices as our spiritual act of worship. We want to begin our time tonight paying some attention to the posture and disposition of our physical bodies when we participate in singing worship together."

Posture check – "Please stand with me, placing your feet about shoulder width apart. Stand tall, but do not lock your knees, and try not to become stiff. Allow your arms to hang loosely from your shoulders. Shake your arms and hands as if shaking off sand. Raise your arms in the air as if touching the sky, then bring them down and allow them to hang to your sides again."

Breathing check – "Stand tall again and inhale through your nose, filling your lungs comfortably with air. Hold the air for about ten seconds and then exhale through your mouth making a small opening as if blowing out a candle. Place one hand on your midsection at about the point of your sternum. Repeat the inhale motion, hold the air for fifteen seconds, and exhale as before through a small opening of your lips. Be aware of the movement that occurs naturally as you inhale and exhale. The movement you should feel is at or below your hand placed on your midsection. It takes air supply to sing, and we want our supply of air to be fresh and sufficient supply."

Sing for fun – "Let's sing a bit and try to be aware of our posture and breath support as we do. We are going to sing a fun song so that you can focus on what is happening with your body. How about singing, 'Twinkle, Twinkle Little Star?'" Sing through in a lower key first, and then move

2 Brian Wren *Praying Twice: The Music and Words of Congregational Song* (Louisville, KY: Westminster John Knox Press, 2000), 84.

up a whole step. Try to enjoy this exercise and encourage singers that they are doing well. Positive and spirited atmosphere is important to the effectiveness of the rehearsal.

A look at music – Perhaps lead singers in prayer before turning to the first music piece. Call attention to the way singing works in our worship encouraging one another, announcing our praise, and shaping how we think about God. Sing (best to begin with something familiar) a song. Evaluate what you are hearing and make appropriate encouragements.

Move through the rehearsal list in predetermined order – Be sure to listen more than sing yourself. As leader in this situation, you need to be in a position to evaluate what you see and hear in regard to the level of participation, posture, and spirit in the singing. If you note people not singing, work toward bringing them into the singing by personal words of encouragement, and possibly by having singers turn to speak words of encouragement to one another.

Be sure to leave time at the end of the singing for prayer and commitment to apply principles learned through the rehearsal. It is also important to draw people's attention to how songs will be used in the dialogue of worship. This admonition accomplishes worship education as well as encourages stronger participation in singing.

Chapter 10
STAYING IN TUNE

Come, Thou Fount of every blessing
Tune my heart to sing Thy grace
Streams of mercy never ceasing
Call for songs of loudest praise
Teach me some melodious sonnet
Sung by flaming tongues above.
Praise the mount! I'm fixed upon it,
Mount of Thy redeeming love.[1]

This text from the eighteenth century preacher, Robert Robinson, has much to say to us about singing our worship in tune. The text relentlessly calls us back to God, the only source of tuning that will result in worship singing that is pleasing to Him. In this sense, it is a superior worship song as it speaks revelation of God's character to us at the same time it gives us means of response. The lyric is an obvious prayer calling upon the Lord to "come." Far too often, our singing begins without an invitation or invocation of the presence and help of the "Fount of every blessing." Such a startup of singing is grossly presumptuous. Ironically,

1 Robert Robinson, "Come, Thou Fount of Every Blessing," in *Baptist Hymnal 2008,* #98.

we may presume the blessing will come regardless. It is precisely that presumptive spirit that may signal that our heart is *out* of tune. Our arrogance may give away the presumption that God is impressed with our singing and that this somehow qualifies as worship that will please Him. To the contrary, our prideful spirit has no place in God-centered worship, except to be sacrificed upon the altar of His glory. If our worship singing is to be renewed, it must surely shun any arrogance or pride. Our prayer must be for the Lord to act and "renew a right spirit within me" (Ps 51:10). A first step toward our heart tuning may be as simple as positioning ourselves to receive His blessing through our confession and faith in His forgiveness. Recognizing our need and surrendering our pride and arrogance that we may sing and serve with true humility are central to singing with hearts in tune. The trust placed in the Giver of blessing and song is a necessary ingredient to sing in tune with the Lord's grace that has come to us freely, unearned.

The next line's reference to eternal "streams of mercy" (Rev 21:6) again indicates a characteristic of the Lord that no doubt "calls for songs of loudest praise." Our need for Him to "teach me some melodious sonnet sung by flaming tongues above" holds potential to move us beyond petty attempts to determine the church's song by selecting music to please our own aesthetic desires, and rather to allow His work in our hearts to unveil a life "sonnet" that would reflect Who Christ is as His work is done in us. Our lives are fixed on the mount of His redemption in love. In Robinson's text, our attention and affection are returned to the Lord Himself. This is theocentric worship.

Here I raise mine Ebenezer
Hither by Thy help I'm come
And I hope by Thy good pleasure
Safely to arrive at home
Jesus sought me when a stranger
Wandering from the fold of God
He to rescue me from danger
Interposed His precious blood

While some contemporary hymnals changed the first line lyric of this second stanza, the biblical reference of 1 Samuel 7:12 that is Robinson's original text seems more poetically rich.[2] Returning to our Ebenezer, our "stone of help," serves as a reminder of God's ongoing help that has brought us to our current state. Our hope to arrive "at home" safely continues the imagery of our journey of faith rested in God's providence. The language is rich with symbolic significance in showing that God was in action when "Jesus sought me when a stranger," while we were aimless in our "wandering from the fold of God." The song helps us express the testimony of our redemption, which again resides not in what we did on our own, but in what He did when He rescued us when He "interposed His precious blood."

Not only is this text full in the testimony it gives, but it's also full in its relentless directing of our grasp of God's work in our redemption. The final stanza included in most hymnals erupts in a prayer-filled dedication that springs from a heart filled with gratitude tempered by a self-awareness that only God's grace ("Thy goodness") will hold it from destruction.

O to grace how great a debtor
Daily I'm constrained to be
Let Thy goodness like a fetter
Bind my wandering heart to Thee
Prone to wander, Lord I feel it
Prone to leave the God I love
Here's my heart, Lord take and seal it
Seal it for Thy courts above

Our hearts are in tune when the Lord Himself has sealed them for His courts. No one else can accomplish this feat. Attempts to fake it ring hollow and ultimately display our inclination to deviate from singing in tune. The lyrics speak truth; we *are* "prone to wander." Hearts singing in concert tuned by the Master tuner make the most glorious music of both immediate and eternal value. It is not that the music is improved by sonic standards, but rather that the resonance of unified spirits worshiping through singing in "spirit and truth" project authentic heart worship. *Benefits* of such singing are immeasurable. Some of those benefits are immediate, humanly enriching, and spiritually gratifying in a way that dwarfs any manipulated thrill. Some benefits are time-released, life giving, path enlightening, and hope protracting that could never be imitated by

2 For example, the popular *Celebration Hymnal* (©1997 Word/Integrity) uses the phrase, "Hitherto Thy love has blest me."

any cheap emotional or intellectual counterfeit. Throughout our singing lives, the attractiveness is never our worship, or our singing itself, but rather always the Christ who is subject and object of our worship singing.

As a church musician and administrator, I have known the frustration of having expensive instruments tuned only to experience some weather change or other factor that causes a loss of intonation. For the worshiping singer, it is important not to become complacent with a heart tuning, lest circumstances or poor choices create the kinds of changes that metaphorically turn our heart's tuning key and bend the pitch that would throw melody and harmony into discord. Many a Christian has experienced spiritual refreshment only to find that the next bend in the road threw them for a proverbial loop and stole the joy in the song of the freshly tuned heart. As previously discussed, many a congregation has experienced the disunity that comes from allowing stylistic preference to supersede *koinonia*. The practice of spiritual disciplines—praying, Scripture reading, fasting, engagement in biblically sound worship and fellowship—are contributors to maintaining tune, though certainly no guarantee. The human heart must remain pliable and accessible to the Holy Spirit for a life of spiritual music-making. Yielding our tuning keys to the Spirit of God better places us in a position to act out our worship through servant ministry.

We never know what ministry awaits us or what life circumstance may be lurking round the corner. I have observed firsthand those whose song crumbled in the pressure of life circumstance, and I have also heard the most beautiful music sung in the midst of impossible situations. As believers we must recognize that we sing worship during lament just as we do during elation.

I stood in the doorway of the hospital nursery, unable to fully commit myself to step all the way into the emotion-packed environment. As her minister of music, I came to visit a choir member and Christian mom who was at the center of the room that was normally filled with healthy babies and a mixture of doting parents, grandparents, and nurses. In this case, Linda sat at the center of the room, singing to her eight-month-old, Melissa, who was fighting for the final breaths she would take on this earth. An apparent victim of the much-publicized Times Beach, Missouri, toxic waste debacle, little Melissa had struggled for half of her short life with an ever increasing number of tumors that riddled her tiny body until this day when the battle with the cancer would come to an end, and her healing would take place by her transition from this life into the arms of Jesus. Though the year was 1980, I readily recall the sights and sounds of that day.

Above the sounds of the occasional sniffling by some of the family members and hospital personnel gathered in the nursery, I could hear the creak of the rocking chair in which Linda sat holding her first and only child. I also heard the familiar strains of the hymn most often identified with small children, "Jesus Loves Me, This I Know." Linda, though afflicted with a severe speech impediment herself, was singing the love of Jesus to her precious baby girl. Linda's condition, coupled with the emotional fog she sang through, made the words nearly unintelligible. However, the sweet tones of a mother's heart cry clearly communicated the powerful message of faith expressed by this mom who was weary from the strain of her baby's suffering, yet was strengthened by God's promise of eternal love. When Linda came to the phrase, "little ones to Him belong, they are weak, but He is strong," I completely lost my composure. I did not want to embarrass the family, or in any way interrupt this sacred moment, so I started to step away. Then I noted that Linda ceased her singing, unable to continue. I prayed, "Lord, give me strength," and began to sing the refrain, "Yes, Jesus loves me. Yes, Jesus loves me." Before I reached the end of that phrase, Lewis, dad and husband, joined the song. Next, a few of the nurses joined, and even the pediatrician who had discouraged the faith element in this family's journey added her voice to the others singing for the brokenhearted mom.

There is power intrinsic to musical expression. During times of heightened emotional sensitivity, music has a way of speaking into our lives and giving unique expression to the highest moments of celebration, the lowest depressions of the human spirit, or the common experiences that define an average day.

Music connects us to times when God has demonstrated His power and may assure us of His dependability for present and future anomalies. On the Sunday following 9/11, I vividly recall singing "O God, Our Help in Ages Past, Our Hope for Years to Come." Isaac Watts' metrical version of Psalm 90:1–5, sung to the strong St. Anne tune, allowed all age groups to participate in declaring assured faith as believers. I found deep solace in joining Christian brothers and sisters in singing that song in the face of the 9/11 tragedy while considering that this same text and tune had been sung in American churches through the days of the Civil War, World Wars I and II, and the Great Depression. Music connects us as the "many members of one body," and helps to form us into community. It provides a means in public worship whereby we can minister to one another and proclaim our witness to the Gospel, while at the same time receiving the ministry of our gathered community's song.

There is an awful lot of "bad news" these days. The hymn writer is right to call us, "Come, Christians, Join to Sing." Our days call for the comforting strains of "Jesus Loves Me," and the reminder of our constant Deliverer who has been our "help in ages past." This is a good time to demonstrate our Christian perspective by what we sing, what we listen to in our everyday life, and what we share with others who may be more open than ever before to the resounding message of sweet assurance, "Yes, Jesus loves me, the Bible tells me so." Worship singing that is empowered by Holy Spirit power will convey the inclusive nature of the "me" that is referenced in that child-friendly song.

Lest we be misunderstood to be a sort of happy time religion, our singing must include the song of lament that may not make us feel better, but rather may express our faith in God despite our time of distress. Music that truly ministers is not just emotionally warm, nor is it always celebrative. To be genuinely effective it must remain true to the Word of God. It must allow for honest, genuine expression in its particular setting, allowing those singing it to do so with integrity. The mystery of the singing's numinous renewal in Christian worship, however, is likely only to become a reality as we allow our singing to be tuned by the One who has given the ability to sing. Our collective song is strengthened as we allow our hearts to be drawn together to "join in a song with sweet accord, and thus surround the throne."[3] Our singing is fine-tuned as "adoration leaves no room for pride"[4] and we move toward the time when we cast our crowns at the feet of the Worthy Lamb and sing with all the saints, "lost in wonder, love and praise."[5]

Soli Deo Gloria!

---

3 Isaac Watts, "We're Marching to Zion" in *Baptist Hymnal,1991,* #524.

4 Fred Pratt Green, "When in Our Music God is Glorified" in *Baptist Hymnal, 1991,* #435.

5 Charles Wesley, "Love Divine, All Loves Excelling" in *Baptist Hymnal, 1991,* #208.

Selected Sources

Akin, Daniel L., ed. *A Theology for the Church.* Nashville: B&H Publishers, 2007.

Ashcraft, Morris. "Revelation" in *The Broadman Bible Commentary.* Nashville: Broadman Press, 1972.

Basden, Paul and David S. Dockery, *The People of God: Essays on the Believer's Church* (Eugene, OR: Wipf & Stock Publishers, 2009).

Bateman, Herbert. *Authentic Worship: Hearing Scripture's Voice, Applying the Truth.* Grand Rapids, MI: Kregel Academic & Professional, 2002.

Begbie, Jeremy S. *Resounding Truth: Christian Wisdom in the World of Music.* Grand Rapids, MI: Baker Academic, 2007.

_______. *Theology, Music, and Time.* New York: Cambridge University Press, 2000.

Beale, G.K. *We Become What We Worship: A Biblical Theology of Idolatry.* Downers Grove, IL: 2008.

Bell, John L. *The Singing Thing: A Case for Congregational Song.* Chicago: GIA Publications, Inc., 2000.

Best, Harold M. *Music Through the Eyes of Faith.* New York: Harper Publishers, 1993.

_______. *Unceasing Worship: Biblical Perspectives on Worship and the Arts.* Downers Grove, IL: Intervarsity Press, 2003.

Blevins, James L. "Introduction to 1 Corinthians" in *Review & Expositor* 80, 1983), 317- 325.

Blomberg, Craig L. *Matthew* in *New American Commentary.* Nashville: Broadman, 1992.

Bonhoeffer, Dietrich. *Life Together: The Classic Exploration of Life in Community.* San Francisco: Harper & Row, 1954.

Bonhoeffer, Dietrich. *Psalms: The Prayer Book of the Bible.* Minneapolis: Augsburg Press, 1970.

Borchert, Gerald. *John 1–11* in *New American Commentary.* Nashville: Broadman & Holman, 1996.

_______. *New Testament Reflections on Worship: Divine Glory and Human Response.* Morristown, TN: Chalice Press, 2007.

Brown, Frank Burch. "Christian Music: More than Just Words," in *Theology Today 62,* (2005).

Bruce, F. F. *The Epistles to the Colossians, Philemon and the Ephesians* in *The New International Commentary on the New Testament.* Grand Rapids, MI: Eerdmans Publishing, 1984.

Brueggemann, Walter. *The Message of the Psalms: a Theological Commentary.* Minneapolis, MN: Augsburg Press, 1984.

Calvin Institute of Worship. http://www.calvin.edu/worship

Carson, Donald A. ed. *From Sabbath to Lord's Day: A Biblical, Historical, and Theological Investigation.* Grand Rapids: Zondervan, 1982; Eugene, OR: Wipf and Stock Publishing, 1999.

_______. *Matthew, Mark, Luke* in *The Expositors Bible Commentary*, volume 8. Grand Rapids, MI: Zondervan, 1984.

_______, Mark Ashton, R. Kent Hughes, and Timothy Keller. *Worship by the Book.* Grand Rapids, MI: Zondervan, 2002.

Conner, W. T. *The Gospel of Redemption.* Nashville: Broadman, 1943.

Clowney, Edmund P. *The Church.* Downers Grove, IL: InterVarsity, 1995.

Corbitt, J. Nathan. *The Sound of the Harvest: Music's Mission in Church and Culture.* Grand Rapids, MI: Baker Books, 1998.

Dawn, Marva. *A Royal Waste of Time: The Splendor of Worshiping God and Being Church for the World.* Grand Rapids, MI: Eerdmans Publishing, 1999.

_______. *How Shall We Worship? Biblical Guidelines for the Worship Wars.* Carol Stream, IL: Tyndale House, 2003.

_______. *Reaching Out without Dumbing Down: A Theology of Worship for the Turnof-the-Century-Culture.* Grand Rapids: Eerdmans, 1995.Dever, Mark E. "The Church" in *A Theology for the Church.* Nashville, TN: B&H Academic, 2007.

Dockery, David S. *Southern Baptist Consensus and Renewal: A Biblical, Historical, and Theological Proposal* Nashville: Broadman & Holman Publishing, 2008)

Doran, Carol and Thomas H. Troeger. *Trouble at the Table: Gathering the Tribes for Worship.* Nashville: Abingdon Press, 1992.

Drane, John. *The McDonaldization of the Church.* Macon, GA: Smyth & Helwys Publishing, 2000.

Eskew, Harry and Hugh T. McElrath. *Singing with Understanding: An Introduction to Christian Hymnology.* Nashville: Broadman Press, 1980.

Frame, John. *Contemporary Worship Music: A Biblical Defense.* Phillipsburg, NJ: P&R Publishing, 1997.

Foley, Edward. "The Cantor in Historical Perspective," *Worship 56:3* (May 1982), 194- 213.

Frankforter, A. Daniel. *Stones for Bread: A Critique of Contemporary Worship.* Louisville, KY: John Knox Press, 2001.

Furr, Gary and Milburn Price. *The Dialogue of Worship: Creating Space for Revelation and Response.* Macon, GA: Smyth & Helwys, 1998.

Garland, David E. *I Corinthians* in *Baker Exegetical Commentary on the New Testament.* Grand Rapids, MI: Baker Academic, 2003.

Garrot, James Leo. *Baptist Theology: A Four Century Study.* Nashville: B&H, 2009.

Grenz, Stanley J. *Theology for the Community of God.* Grand Rapids, MI: Eerdmans Publishing, 2000.

Grout, Donald Jay. *A History of Western Music,* third edition. New York: Norton & Company, 1980.

Hammett, John. *Biblical Foundations for Baptist Churches: A Contemporary Ecclesiology.* Grand Rapids, MI: Kregel Academics & Professional, 2005.

Hawn, C. Michael. *Gather Into One: Praying and Singing Globally.* Grand Rapids, MI: Eerdmans Publishing, 2003.

Herr, Kathryn and Gary L. Anderson. *The Action Research Dissertation: A Guide for Students and Faculty.* Thousand Oaks, CA: Sage Publications, 2005.

Herring, Reuben. *Valleys, Plateaus, Peaks: A 170 Year History of First Baptist Church Nashville, Tennessee.* Nashville: First Baptist Church Nashville, TN, 1990.

Hielema, Syd. "The Festival Envy Syndrome: Four Contexts for Worship" *Reformed Worship, 71,* March 2004.

Hill, Andrew E. *Enter His Courts with Praise: Old Testament Worship for the New Testament Church.* Grand Rapids, MI: Baker Books, 1996.

Hustad, Donald. *Jubilate II: Church Music in Worship and Renewal.* Carol Stream, IL: Hope Publishing, 1993.

Jamieson, Robert and Andrew Fausset and David Brown. *A Commentary: Critical, Experimental, and Practical on the Old and New Testaments.* Grand

Rapids, MI: Eerdmans, 1993. Reproduced in *PC Study Bible 5* [CD-ROM] (Seattle, WA: Biblesoft, 2006.

Johansson, Calvin M. *Music & Ministry: A Biblical Counterpoint.* Peabody MA: Hendrickson Publishers, 1984.

Kidd, Reggie M. *With One Voice: Discovering Christ's Song in Our Worship.* Grand Rapids, MI: Baker Books, 2005.

Kuhne, Gary W. and B. Allan Quigley. "Understanding and Using Action Research in

Practice Settings" in *New Directions for Adult and Continuing Education,* no. 73 (Spring, 1997).

Leonard, Bill J. *Baptists in America.* New York: Columbia University Press, 2005.

Lewis, C. S. *The Weight of Glory.* San Francisco: Harper San Francisco, 2001.

Long, Thomas G. *Beyond the Worship Wars: Building Vital and Faithful Worship.* Bethesda, MD: Alban Institute, 2000.

May, Lynn Jr. *The First Baptist Church of Nashville, Tennessee, 1820–1970.* Nashville: First Baptist Church Nashville, Tennessee, 1970.

McKee, Elsie. "Calvin: The Form of Church Prayers, Strasbourg Liturgy (1545)" in *The Complete Library of Christian Worship,* ed. Robert Webber, Nashville: Starsong, 1994, 195–198.

McBeth, H. Leon. *The Baptist Heritage: Four Centuries of Baptist Witness.* Nashville, TN: Broadman Press, 1987.

Meyer, Leonard M. *Emotion and Meaning in Music.* Chicago: University of Chicago Publishing, 1956.

Mitman, F. Russell. *Worship in the Shape of Scripture.* Cleveland: The Pilgrim Press, 2001.

Navarro, Kevin J. *The Complete Worship Leader.* Grand Rapids, MI: Baker Books, 2001.

Nelson, David P. "Voicing God's Praise" in *Authentic Worship,* ed. Herbert W. Bateman IV. Grand Rapids, MI: Kregel Academic & Professional, 2002.

Otto, Rudolf. *The Idea of the Holy.* London: Oxford University Press, 1923.

Patton, John. *Pastoral Care in Context: an Introduction to Pastoral Care.* Louisville, KY: John Knox Press, 1993.

Pavlicevic, Mercedes. *Music Therapy in Context: Music, Meaning and Relationship.* London: Jessica Kingsley Publishers Ltd, 1997, second printing 2000.

Payne, Leanne. *Healing Presence: Curing the Soul through Union with Christ.* Grand Rapids, MI: Baker Books, 1995.

_______. *Real Presence: The Glory of Christ with Us and Within Us.* Grand Rapids, MI: Baker Books, 1995.

Peterson, David K. *Engaging with God: A Biblical and Theological Foundation for Worship.* Downers Grove, IL: InterVarsity Press, 1992.

Peterson, Eugene. *Christ Plays in Ten Thousand Places.* Grand Rapids, MI: William B. Eerdmans, 2005.

Plantinga Jr., Cornelius, and Sue A. Rozeboom. *Discerning the Spirits: A Guide to Thinking about Christian Worship Today.* Grand Rapids: Eerdmans Publishing, 2003.

Putnam, Robert D. *Bowling Alone: The Collapse and Revival of American Community.*

New York: Simon & Schuster Paperbacks, 2000.

Ralston, Timothy J. "Scripture in Worship" in *Authentic Worship: Hearing Scripture's Voice, Applying Its Truths.* Grand Rapids, MI: Kregel Academic and Professional, 2002.

Richardson, Paul. "Spiritual Formation in Christian Worship," *Review & Expositor* 96, 1999.

Roberts, Vaughan. *True Worship.* Carlisle, UK: 2001.

Ruth, Lester. "*Lex Amandi, Lex Orandi*: The Trinity in the Most Used Contemporary Christian Worship Songs," Prepared for and delivered at a conference entitled "The Place of Christ in Liturgical Prayer: Christology, Trinity, and Liturgical Theology," Yale Institute of Sacred Music, February 27, 2005.

Saliers, Don. *Music and Theology*. Nashville, TN: Abingdon Press, 2007.

_______, *Worship as Theology: Foretaste of Glory Divine*. Nashville: Abingdon Press, 1994.

Schmuck, Richard A. *Practical Action Research for Change*. Arlington Heights, IL: Skylight Professional Development, 1997.

Stapert, Calvin R. *A New Song in an Old World*. Grand Rapids, MI: Eerdmans Publishing, 2007.

Stone, Howard W., and James O. Duke. *How to Think Theologically*. Minneapolis: Fortress Press, 2006.

Stuart, David K. *Exodus* in *The New American Bible Commentary*. Nashville: Broadman & Holman, 2003.

The Worship Sourcebook. Grand Rapids, MI: Baker Books, 2004.

Thornbury, Gregory Allen. "Prolegomena: Introduction to the Task of Theology" in *A Theology for the Church* ed. Daniel L. Akin, 2–69. Nashville: Broadman & Holman Academics, 2007.

Torrance, James B. *Community & the Triune God of Grace*. Downers Grove, IL: InterVarsity Press, 1996.

Tozer, A. W. *Whatever Happened to Worship? A Call to True Worship*. Camp Hill, PA: Christian Publications, 1985

Trentham, Charles A. *Broadman Bible Commentary: Hebrews*. Nashville: Broadman Publishing, 1972.

Van Dyk, Leanne, ed. *A More Profound Alleluia: Theology and Worship in Harmony*. Grand Rapids: Eerdman's Publishing, 2005

Watts, John D., John Joseph Owens, and Marvin E. Tate, Jr. "Job" in *The Broadman Bible Commentary. Nashville: Broadman Press, 1971.*

Webber, Robert E. *Ancient-Future Faith: Rethinking Evangelicalism for a Postmodern World.* Grand Rapids, MI: Baker Books, 1999.

_______. *The Divine Embrace: Recovering the Passionate Spiritual Life.* Grand Rapids, MI: Baker Books, 2006.

_______. *Ancient-Future Worship: Proclaiming and Enacting God's Narrative.* Grand Rapids: Baker Books, 2008.

_______. "The Crisis in Evangelical Worship," in *Ancient and Postmodern Christianity: Paleo-Orthodoxy in the 21st Century,* Kenneth Tanner and Christopher A. Hall, ed. Downers Grove, IL: InterVarsity Press, 2002.

_______ *Worship Old & New.* Grand Rapids, MI: Zondervan, 1994.

Weiss, Piero, and Richard Taruskin. *Music in the Western World: A History in Document.* Belmont, CA: Wadsworth Group/Thomson Learning, 1984.

Westermeyer, Paul. "Here, Now, and Beyond," in *The Hymn*, Vol. 54, No. 1, (January, 2003).

_______. *Te Deum: The Church and Music.* Minneapolis: Fortress Press, 1998.

Wilken, Robert "The Church's Way of Speaking," In *First Things: A Monthly Journal of Religious and Public Life.* Issue 155, (August/September 2005).

Willimon, William H. *Worship as Pastoral Care.* Nashville: Abingdon Press, 1979.

Wilson-Dickson, Andrew. *The Story of Christian Music: From Gregorian Chant to Black Gospel, An Illustrated Guide to All the Major Traditions of Music in Worship.* Minneapolis: Fortress Press, 2003.

Winter, Richard. *Still Bored in a Culture of Entertainment.* Downers Grove, IL:

InterVarsity Press, 2002.

Wren, Brian. *Praying Twice: The Music and Words of Congregational Song.* Louisville, KY: Westminster John Knox Press, 2000.

Wren, Brian. "Sing It, Preacher!' Thoughts about Contemporary Worship Music," in *Journal for Preachers, 24.01* (Advent 2000)

Yee, Russell. "Shared Meaning and Significance in Congregational Singing," *The Hymn,* Vol. 48, No. 2 (April, 1997): 7–11

York, Terry W. *American Worship Wars.* Peabody, MA: Hendrickson Publishers, 2003.

York, Terry W., and David Bolin. *The Voice of Our Congregation.* Nashville: Abingdon Press, 2005.

LaVergne, TN USA
28 February 2011
218108LV00003B/2/P